Diabetic Cookbook for the Newly Diagnosed

Table of Contents

Introduction 13
Part 1: Your Daily Favorites 14
Chapter 1: Delicious Wake Up Ideas 14
  Bagels 14
  Banana-Carrot & Pecan Muffins 16
  Pancake Option 18
    Cottage Cheese Pancakes 18
    Meal Prep Pancakes 20
    Pumpkin Pancakes 21
  Other Breakfast/Brunch Favorites 23
    Apple-Spiced Overnight Oats 23
    Asparagus Omelet 24
    Baked Eggs 25
    BBQ Deviled Eggs with Turkey Bacon 26
    Breakfast Burrito 28
    Breakfast Quinoa 30
    Chicken & Zucchini Omelet 32
    Crispy Egg Cups 33
    Egg White Scrambled Egg with Cherry Tomatoes & Spinach 35
    Ham & Egg Cups 37
    Kale & Goat Cheese Frittata 39
    Poached Eggs 41

Shrimp Toast 42
Zucchini Nest Eggs 44
Chapter 2: Tasty Smoothies 45
Make a Freezer Smoothie Pack 45
Smoothies in a Bowl 47
Almond-Mango Smoothie 47
Berry Smoothie 48
Other Delicious Favorites 49
Banana-Strawberry Smoothie 49
Carrot Smoothie 50
Delicious Coffee & Oats Smoothie 51
Extra Green Smoothie – Option One 52
Extra-Green Avocado Smoothie – Option Two 53
Grapefruit-Pineapple Detox Smoothie 54
Green Tea Fruit Smoothie 55
Mango-Raspberry Smoothie 56
Minty Berry Kefir Smoothie 57
Oatmeal Breakfast Smoothie 58
Peanut Butter – Chocolate & Banana Smoothie 59
Pineapple-Strawberry Smoothie 60
Strawberry Smoothie 61
Vegan Avocado-Chocolate Smoothie 62
Chapter 3: Fruity & Nut Favorites 63

Almond-Stuffed Dates 63
Berry Crumble 64
Chili-Lime Grilled Pineapple 66
Flavorful Marinated Oranges 67
Maple Apples 68
Mini Apple Chimichanga 70
Picnic Berry Shortcakes 72
Warm & Spicy Apples 74
Nuts & Berries with Whipped Cheese 75

Part 2: Air Fryer Meal Favorites 76

Chapter 4: Chicken Time 76

Breast of Chicken 76
Chicken Meatballs 78
Chicken Nuggets 80
Chicken Thighs 82
Crispy Cornish Hen 83
Crumbly Tenderloin of Chicken 84
Frozen Chicken Patties 85
Jamaican Fajitas 86
Lemon Pepper Chicken Breast 87
Southwestern-Style Chicken Fajitas 88
Sweet Chili Wings 90
Turkey Meatballs 92
Veggies & Chicken 93

Chapter 5: Pork Time 95

Broccoli & Chops 95

Pork Bites 97

Pork Chops – Breaded 98

Pork Chops – Ranch-Style 100

Pork Steaks 101

Chapter 6: Seafood Time 102

Shrimp Favorites 102

Air-Fried Dragon Shrimp 102

Breaded Fried Shrimp 103

Chinese-Cuisine Garlic Prawns 105

Coconut Shrimp 106

Other Seafood Options 108

Basil & Tomato Scallops 108

Fried Rice & Sriracha Salmon 111

Fried Salmon Cakes 113

Frozen Fish 114

Salmon Fillets 115

Swordfish Kebabs 116

Chapter 7: Side Dish Favorites 117

Asparagus 117

Bacon-Brussels Sprouts 118

Baked Potatoes with Broccoli & Cheese 120

Breaded Eggplant 122

Breaded Mushrooms 124

Brussels Sprouts 125

Cabbage Favorite 126

Delicious Corn-on-the-Cob 127

Mixed Veggies 128

Polenta Fries 130

Sweet Potato Fries 131

Veggie Frittata with Cheese 132

Part 3: Meal Favorites - Other Methods 133

Chapter 8: Noodles & Other Specialties 133

Baked Zucchini Noodles with Cheese 133

Cabbage Patties 135

Caprese Skewers 136

Cauliflower Fried Rice 137

Cauliflower Hash Browns 138

'Cauliflower Mac' & Cheese 139

Edamame Kelp Noodles 141

Luncheon Cauliflower & Spinach Bowl 142

Philly Cheesesteak Stuffed Peppers 144

Red Pepper Zoodles 146

Vegetarian Sautéed Zucchini with Tomatoes 147

Chapter 9: Other Favorite Meals 148

Soup Options 148

Burger Stew 148

Cauliflower Beef Curry 150

Colby Cauliflower Soup & Pancetta Chips 151

Creamy Chicken Soup 153

Creamy Pumpkin & Sausage Chowder 154

Curried-Style Fish Stew 156

Egg Drop Soup 158

Green Chicken Enchilada Soup 160

Green Soup 161

Mushroom-Kale & Sausage Soup 162

Pumpkin Soup 163

Shirataki Soup 165

Spicy Cauliflower Soup 166

Salad Favorites 168

Avocado & Tomato Salad Specialty 168

Balsamic Blackberry & Spinach Salad 169

Brussel Sprout Salad 170

Caprese Salad 171

Chicken & Apple Creamy-Style Salad 172

Chicken & Berry Salad 173

Chicken-Pecan Salad & Cucumber Bites 174

Chopped Greek Salad 175

Cucumber Avocado Salad 176

Curry Egg Salad 178
Greek Lamb Meatball Salad 179
Green Bean Balsamic Salad 181
Green Salad with Beets & Edamame 183
Jar Salad on the Go for Vegans 184
Lobster Salad 185
Mustard Sardines Salad 186
Niçoise Salad 187
Rosemary Tomato Salad 189
Scallion & Snap Pea Salad 190
Shrimp & Avocado Salad 191
Tuna Salad & Chives 192

Dressing & Condiment Options 193
Alfredo Sauce 193
Avocado Sauce 194
BBQ Sauce 195
Brown Gravy with Zero Carbs 196
Caesar Dressing 197
Classic Guacamole 198
Creamy Mushroom Sauce 199
Enchilada Sauce 200
Garlic-Parmesan Wing Sauce 201
Marinara Sauce 202
Mayonnaise 203
No-Cook Avocado Hollandaise 204

    Onion Gravy for Meat 205

    Pesto-Basil Sauce 207

    Ranch Seasoning Mix 208

    Tahini Dressing 209

    White Wine Mustard 210

  Vinaigrette Options 211

    Asian Vinaigrette 211

    Balsamic Vinaigrette 212

    Citrus Vinaigrette 213

Part 4: Dessert & Beverage Specialties 214

Chapter 10: Diabetic Desserts 214

  Cakes 214

    Cappuccino Cupcake Delight 214

  Cookies & Fudge 216

    Banana Chocolate Chip Cookies 216

    Carrot Cookie Bites 218

    Chocolate Kiss & Peanut Butter Cookie Treats 220

    Easy & Light Cookie Cut-Outs 221

    Molasses-Crackle Cookies 223

    Peanut Butter & Oatmeal Cookies 225

  Bar Type Cakes 226

    Almond Espresso Bars 226

    Fudge 228

Pies & Tarts 229
- Apple Pie 229
- Deconstructed Raspberry Pie 231
- Ginger Plum Tart 232
- Key Lime Pie 234
- Ribbon Pudding Pie 235

Tasty Sweet Treats 237
- No-Bake Peanut Butter Treats 237
- Sour Cream Bavarian 238

Delicious Frozen Treats 240
- Apricot Lemon Fruit Pops 240
- Berry Ice Pops 241
- Berry Yogurt Swirls 242
- Chocolate Hazelnut & Soy Pops 243
- Chunky Banana Cream Freeze 244
- Patriotic Pops 245
- Soft-Serve Raspberry-Banana 247
- Rhubarb- Strawberry Ice Pops 248
- Strawberry Lemonade Popsicles 250
- Strawberry Sorbet 251

Chapter 11: Diabetic Favorite Beverages 253
- Agua-&-Strawberry Fresca 253
- Basil Lemonade 254
- Citrusy Spa Water 255

Healthy Fruit Sparklers 256

Lemon & Ginger Tea 257

Sunrise Peach Refresher 258

Chapter 12: Diabetic Mocktails & Cocktails 259

Blood Orange Margaritas 259

Ginger-Lemon Kombucha Cocktail 261

Hot Bourbon Cocoa 262

Mojito Mocktails 263

Spicy Ginger-Pineapple Mocktail 264

Spicy Hot Cider & Apple Brandy 265

The Final Words to Satisfaction 266

A Healthy Avocado Bowl 266

Avocado Toast 267

Nut Butter & Sliced Apples 267

Nut Butter Whole Grain Toast 267

Guacamole & Raw Veggies 267

Hard-Boiled Eggs 268

Celery & Peanut Butter 268

Cucumber Boats 268

Edamame Favorite 268

Fruit & Cheese 268

Green Wrap 269

Ranch & Raw Veggies 269

Savory Cottage Cheese 269

Sweet Cottage Cheese 269

Cream Cheese & Cucumber Sandwiches 270

Hummus & Raw Veggies 270

Peanut Butter & Chocolate 270

Peanut Butter Sandwich Crackers 270

Popcorn Favorite 270

Roasted Chickpeas 271

Trail Mix 271

Turkey Cheese Wrap 271

Savory Yogurt Parfait 271

Yogurt Parfait 272

Introduction

I hope you will enjoy each segment of *Diabetic Cookbook for the Newly Diagnosed*. It is filled with many delicious recipes with you in mind so you can enjoy your food as you learn which ones you can enjoy without interfering with your Diabetic goals.

You will learn how to prepare breakfast, lunchtime, and dinner meals quickly so you can continue with your busy lifestyle. Each one can be prepared within about one-half an hour.

The Air Fryer was chosen so you can continue to enjoy dining with your family with many of the same foods as always, just prepared differently. You will be using less grease, making each item much healthier.

Even though you will find many recipes using the fryer unit throughout the book, there is a special section for dinner options to save tons of time. You can still enjoy desserts and healthy fruit-oriented snacks for a pleasurable dining experience.

You also have another segment devoted to other methods of meals to prepare easily.

Please enjoy!

Part 1: Your Daily Favorites
Chapter 1: Delicious Wake Up Ideas

Bagels

Servings: 8
Time Required: 15 minutes

Essential Ingredients:

- Flour – all-purpose & unbleached suggested (2 cups)
- Baking powder (1 tbsp.)
- Kosher salt (1 tsp.)
- Greek yogurt – plain (2 cups)
- Eggs (1)

Prep Method:

1. Preheat the fryer to 350° Fahrenheit/177° Celsius.
2. First, whisk the dry components and mix in the yogurt with a plastic/rubber spatula to create a dough ball. Toss it onto a floured surface.
3. Cut the dough into eight portions. Then roll the portions into a 'rope' and pushing the sides together to form the bagel.

4. Whisk the egg and brush the prepared bagels to cook
5. Air fry them till browned as desired (10-12 min.).
6. Wait about five minutes before slicing to serve for the best results.

Banana-Carrot & Pecan Muffins

Servings: 6
Required Time: 30 minutes

Essential Ingredients:

- Kosher salt (.5 tsp.)
- Baking powder (1 tsp.)
- Flour - whole wheat (1 cup)
- Cinnamon - ground (1 tsp.)
- Baking soda (.25 tsp.)
- Brown sugar (.33 cup)
- Large egg (1)
- Vanilla sugar-free yogurt (.33 cup)
- Carrot (.75 cup)
- Banana (.5 cup)
- Vanilla extract (1 tsp.)
- Canola oil (.25 cup)
- Pecans (.25 cup)

Prep Method:

1. Place paper/foil liners in a six-cup muffin tin.
2. Mash the bananas, shred the carrot, and chop the pecans. Set them aside.
3. Whisk the dry fixings (up to the line **) in a big bowl.
4. Then, combine the oil with the sugar and egg in another container. Mix in the yogurt, carrots, banana, and vanilla. Stir

the oil mix into the flour mixture in a big mixing container. Fold in the pecans.
5. Scoop the batter evenly into the muffin cups.
6. Set a timer to bake at 375° Fahrenheit or 191° Celsius until muffins are lightly browned as desired (22 min.).

Pancake Option

You can enjoy your deliciously prepared pancakes for a full day when stored in a closed container in the refrigerator. Before storing pancakes, let them cool fully. If not, the moisture will cause them to become wet. Reheat them in the microwave.

Cottage Cheese Pancakes

Servings: 1 @ 1-2 large
Time Required: 10 minutes

Essential Ingredients:

- Low-fat cottage cheese (.5 cup/110 g)
- Oats (.25 cup/20 g)
- Eggs (2 eggs for 1/3 cup or 90 g – whites only used)
- Vanilla extract (1 tsp.)
- Optional: Stevia in the raw (1 tbsp.) for sweeter cakes

Prep Method:

1. First, pour the cottage cheese and egg whites into the blender, then add the stevia, vanilla, and oats. Blend the fixings till the mixture is velvety.
2. Preheat a skillet (medium heat) and spritz it with a little cooking spray.

3. Then make the pancakes to serve with some sugar-free peanut butter, berries, or jam as desired.

Meal Prep Pancakes

Servings: 4
Time Required: 20 minutes

Essential Ingredients:

- Coconut flour (1 cup)
- Large eggs (8)
- Melted coconut oil (.25 cup)
- Almond milk (1.5 cups/as needed)

Optional Garnishes:
- Strawberries
- Almond butter

Prep Method:

1. Combine all the pancake fixings. Prepare the skillet with a bit of oil as needed.
2. Dispense the batter (2-3 tbsp. each) into the skillet (medium temperature).
3. When done, portion them into containers with diced berries.
4. When serving, enjoy with the desired toppings.

Pumpkin Pancakes

Servings: 6
Time Required: 15-20 minutes

Essential Ingredients:

- Milk (1.5 cups)
- Egg (1)
- Vinegar (2 tbsp.)
- Pumpkin puree (1 cup)
- Vegetable oil (2 tbsp.)
- Baking soda (1 tsp.)
- Flour – okay to use all-purpose (2 cups)
- Allspice - ground (1 tsp.)
- Brown sugar or sugar-free 'Truvia' (3 tbsp.)
- Salt (.5 tsp.)
- Baking powder (2 tsp.)
- Ginger - ground (.5 tsp.)
- Cinnamon (1 tsp.)

Prep Method:

1. Whisk the vinegar, oil, egg, pumpkin, and milk.
2. Combine the dry fixings in another container (baking powder, salt, ginger, cinnamon, allspice, baking soda, brown sugar, and flour).
3. Stir the fixings together.
4. Heat a skillet (medium-high temperature).

5. Scoop the batter into the griddle and brown on both sides. Serve hot.

Other Breakfast/Brunch Favorites

Apple-Spiced Overnight Oats

Servings: 2
Time Required: 5 minutes (+) 2 hours/overnight chilling

Essential Ingredients:

- Hemp hearts (.25 cup/35 g)
- Rolled oats (3 tbsp./20 g)
- Chia seeds (1 tbsp./12 g)
- Cinnamon (1 tsp.)
- Greek yogurt - plain (.25 cup/115 g)
- Shredded apple (.25 cup/25 g)
- Milk (.75 cup/180 g)
- Optional: Pecan halves (6-8)
- Also Needed: 2-cup mason jar/another container

Prep Method:

1. Toss, and shake the cinnamon, chia seeds, oats, and hemp hearts.
2. Fold in the apple and yogurt, add the milk, and stir thoroughly till combined.
3. Pop the jar in the fridge to chill (2 hr. to overnight) but can be kept for up to three days.
4. Before serving, garnish with the pecans.

Asparagus Omelet

Servings: 1
Time Required: 13-15 minutes

Essential Ingredients:

- Eggs (1 whole + 3 whites)
- Asparagus (.5 cup)
- Mushroom (1 medium)
- Low-fat cheddar/your choice cheese (.25 cup + 1 tbsp.)
- Light butter (1 tbsp.)
- Black pepper & salt (as desired)

Prep Method:

1. Whisk all the eggs and whites with seasonings to your liking.
2. Cut the asparagus into ¼-inch slices, keeping the tips whole.
3. Chop the mushrooms. Sauté the asparagus and mushroom in butter (1 tbsp.).
4. Pour the egg mixture into a clean skillet to prepare the omelet. Add the asparagus and mushroom mixture before folding the omelet over.
5. Top with a tablespoon of cheese to serve.

Baked Eggs

Servings: 4
Time Required: 10-12 minutes

Essential Ingredients:

- Large eggs (4)
- Optional: Milk of choice (1 tsp.)
- To Serve: Fresh Herbs - Thyme or chives
- Also Needed: 4 ceramic ramekins @ 4 oz./110 g each

Prep Method:

1. Set the Air Fryer at 300° Fahrenheit/149° Celsius.
2. Lightly mist the inside of the ramekins with a nonstick cooking oil spray.
3. Place the ramekins into the fryer basket.
4. Carefully break one egg into each ramekin, be careful not to break the yolk.
5. If desired, swirl milk or cream (¼ tsp.) into each egg white.
6. Cook until the egg whites are just set (7-10 min.).
7. Use tongs to transfer the ramekins from the fryer.
8. Season with salt, pepper, and fresh herbs as desired.

BBQ Deviled Eggs with Turkey Bacon

Servings: 12
Time Required: 25 minutes

Essential Ingredients:

- Turkey bacon (3 slices)
- Large - hard-boiled eggs (12 peeled)
- Greek yogurt - plain used (.5 cup/140 g)
- BBQ sauce (2 tbsp.)
- Smoked paprika (.5 tsp.)
- Kosher salt (.25 tsp.)
- Dijon mustard (1 tsp.)
- Optional: Freshly chopped chives (.5 tsp.)

Prep Method:

1. Prepare the bacon in a skillet till it is crispy, and add to a layer of towels to drain the fat. When cooled, crumble.
2. Halve the eggs - lengthwise. Scoop the yolks into a mixing container, then place the whites on a serving plate. Mash the yolks using a fork until smooth.
3. Now mix in the yogurt, barbecue sauce, mustard, salt, and paprika, then stir until fully mixed.
4. Pipe/spoon the yolk mixture into the egg white halves.

5. Garnish with crumbles and chives, if using to serve.

Breakfast Burrito

Servings: 6
Time Required: 25 minutes

Essential Ingredients:

- Large eggs (6)
- Whole milk (3 tbsp.)
- Butter (1 tbsp.)
- Black pepper (1 tsp.)
- Low-carb wraps or tortillas (6)
- Cooked bacon (5 oz./150 g)
- Spinach (5 oz.)
- Bell pepper (half of 1)
- Shredded cheese (1 cup/80 g)

Prep Method:

1. First, whisk the eggs and milk with pepper.
2. Prepare a pot of water to prepare the spinach till it is wilted (3-5 min.)
3. Scoop it from the pan and drain thoroughly in a colander for now.
4. Prep a frying pan over medium heat and add the butter.
5. Now add the eggs while stirring occasionally till they are scrambled as desired.
6. Chop the bacon and thinly slice the pepper.

7. Make the burritos in the tortilla with layers of egg, spinach, peppers, and bacon with a garnish of shredded cheese.
8. Spice it up with sauce if you choose and wrap it to serve.

Breakfast Quinoa

Servings: 4
Time Required: 25-30 minutes

Essential Ingredients:

- Raw almonds (.25 cup)
- Cinnamon (1 tsp.)
- Sea salt (1 tsp.)
- Quinoa (1 cup)
- Milk (2 cups)
- Vanilla extract (1 tsp.)
- Honey (2 tbsp.)
- Dried pitted dates (2)
- Dried apricots (5)

Prep Method:

1. Toast the almonds in a skillet until just golden (3-5 min. @ medium) and place to the side for now.
2. Finely chop the apricots, dates, and almonds.
3. Warm the quinoa and cinnamon in a saucepan (medium temperature).
4. Pour in the milk and salt. Wait for it to boil and lower the temperature setting to low. Put a top on the pot to simmer (15 min.).
5. When ready, mix in the dates, apricots, honey, and vanilla. Stir and serve with the rest of the almonds.

6. Note: Since fiber and protein are thought to be crucial for maintaining blood sugar control, quinoa may be especially advantageous for those who have diabetes.

Chicken & Zucchini Omelet

Servings: 2
Time Required: 35 minutes

Essential Ingredients:

- Milk (.5 cup)
- Eggs (8)
- Salt & pepper (to your liking)
- Cooked chicken (1 cup)
- Fresh chives (1 pinch/to taste)
- Zucchini (.75 cup)
- Cheddar cheese - shredded (1 cup)

Prep Method:

1. Heat the Air Fryer to reach 315° Fahrenheit/157° Celsius.
2. Chop the chicken, zucchini, and chives.
3. Whisk the eggs with pepper, salt, and milk.
4. Toss in the rest of the fixings and scoop into a greased baking pan to fit in the Air Fryer unit.
5. Select the cooking time to 35 minutes.
6. When ready, slice into wedges and serve piping hot.

Crispy Egg Cups

Servings: 4
Time Required: 18 minutes

Essential Ingredients:

- Nonstick cooking spray
- Whole wheat bread - toasted (4 slices)
- Trans-fat-free margarine (1.5 tbsp.)
- Deli-style ham (1 slice - about 2 oz./56 g)
- Large eggs (4)
- Salt and black pepper (.125 or 1/8 tsp. each)

Prep Method:

1. Preheat the air fryer (basket in place) to 375° Fahrenheit/191° Celsius.
2. Spray four (8-ounce) oven-proof custard cups or ramekins with nonstick cooking oil spray.
3. Cut the crusts from the bread - spread one side of the bread with the margarine.
4. Place the bread, margarine-side-down into a ramekin and press gently to shape the bread to the cup - till done.
5. Slice the ham into ½-inch strips - arranging them single-layered in the cups. Crack one egg into each cup. Dust it with salt and pepper.

6. Place the filled, uncovered custard cups in the fryer basket. Air fry until the eggs are softly set or done as desired (10-13 min.).
7. Carefully remove the ramekin from the fryer basket and run a knife around the sides to transfer to a plate.

Egg White Scrambled Egg with Cherry Tomatoes & Spinach

Servings: 4
Required Time: 5-10 minutes

Essential Ingredients:

- Garlic (1 clove)
- Fresh baby spinach (2 cups - packed)
- Halved cherry tomatoes (2 cups)
- Eggs (10 egg whites + 1 whole)
- Black pepper (.25 tsp.)
- Salt (.5 tsp.)
- Olive oil (1 tbsp.)
- Light cream/Half & Half (.5 cup)
- Finely grated parmesan cheese (.25 cup)

Prep Method:

1. Prepare a frying pan over medium-high heat setting.
2. Mince and toss the garlic into the pan once it's hot to sauté it (1/2 minute).
3. Stir in the spinach and tomatoes. Continue sauteing for one additional minute until the tomato texture is softened and the spinach has wilted.
4. Whisk the eggs, pepper, salt, and milk. Add the mixture into the pan using the medium heat setting. Fold in the egg and cook it for about two to three minutes.

5. Transfer the pan from the burner and sprinkle it with cheese.

Ham & Egg Cups

Servings: 8
Time Required: 30 minutes

Essential Ingredients:

- Cooked ham (8 thin deli-style slices)
- Mozzarella cheese (.25 cups/1 oz.)
- Eggs (8)
- Optional: Basil (8 tsp.)
- Black pepper (as desired)
- Grape or cherry tomatoes (6)
- Also Needed: Muffin tin (8-count)

Prep Method:

1. Preheat the oven at 350° Fahrenheit/177° Celsius. Coat the muffin tin cups with the spray.
2. Press the ham slice into the bottom and add the cheese to each of the prepared cups.
3. Next, break an egg into the cup and sprinkle with pepper. Add the pesto, if using.
4. Slice the tomatoes into halves and place them on each of the cups.
5. Bake for 18-20 minutes. The egg whites should be set, like a regular poached egg. Leave them in the cups for 3-5 minutes.

6. Lastly, carefully take the cups out of the tin and serve.

Kale & Goat Cheese Frittata

Servings: 6
Time Required: 15-20 minutes

Essential Ingredients:

- Fresh kale (2 torn cups)
- Onion (1 medium)
- Olive oil (2 tsp.)
- Eggs (6)
- Egg whites (4)
- Black pepper (.125 or 1/8 tsp.)
- Salt (.25 tsp.)
- Dried tomatoes (.25 cup)
- Goat cheese (1 oz.)

Prep Method:

1. Thinly slice the onion in half. Drain and thinly slice the tomatoes and crumble the cheese.
2. Warm the oven broiler while you cook the kale and onion (medium @ 10 min.)
3. Whisk the eggs, pepper, and salt. Pour the mix into the skillet using the med-low heat setting.
4. When the edges are almost set, sprinkle it with the tomatoes and cheese.
5. Transfer it to the broiler (4-5 inches from the heat) for one to two minutes.
6. Slice it into six wedges and serve.

7. Note: For those with type 2 diabetes, goat cheese might be the healthiest cheese option.

Poached Eggs

Servings: 2
Time Required: 10-12 minutes

Essential Ingredients:

- Champagne vinegar (1 tsp.)
- Salt (.5 tsp.)
- Fresh eggs (2)

Prep Method:

1. Heat a saucepan over medium heat. Add the cold water and wait for it to boil. Stir in the salt and vinegar.
2. Break each of the eggs into a ramekin. Place it close to the water and slide it out of the dish. Simmer until set.
3. Use a slotted spoon to lift it from the pan to help prevent sticking. Continue cooking until the yolk is runny and the white is cooked for about six minutes.
4. Prepare a container with ice water. Transfer the eggs from the pan to the bowl of ice water (It slows and stops the cooking process.)
5. Drain the poached eggs on a paper towel before serving.

Shrimp Toast

Servings: 4
Time Required: 18-20 minutes

Essential Ingredients:

- Shrimp (.5 lb./230 g)
- Egg (1)
- Cilantro (.5 cup)
- Scallions (2 + more to garnish)
- Cornstarch (2 tsp.)
- Garlic (1 clove)
- Soy sauce (1 tsp.)
- Ginger - peeled (1 tsp.)
- Sandwich bread (4 slices)
- Sesame seeds (.25 cup)

Prep Method:

1. Preheat the Air Fryer to 370° Fahrenheit/188° Celsius for three minutes
2. Peel and devein the shrimp. Thinly slice the scallions - on the diagonal. Chop/mince the cilantro, garlic, and ginger.
3. Use a sharp knife to slice away the crust from the bread slices - cut it into 16 triangles.
4. Whisk the egg and toss with the shrimp, ginger, scallions, garlic, cilantro,

cornstarch, and soy sauce in a food processor.
5. Combine the mix till you have a smooth paste. (It may be lumpy.)
6. Pour the sesame seeds into a platter.
7. Spread the shrimp mixture over the bread triangles.
8. Dip half of the triangles (shrimp side down) in the sesame seeds to cover evenly.
9. Place the bread in the Air Fryer tray (shrimp side up), working in batches if necessary.
10. Set the time for six to eight minutes, checking halfway through the cooking process.
11. Transfer the toast to a serving dish after it's crispy and golden to your liking. Serve it with a garnish of green onion - piping hot.

Zucchini Nest Eggs

Servings: 4
Time Required: 15 minutes

Essential Ingredients:

- Grated zucchini (8 oz./230 g)
- Butter/margarine (4 tsp.)
- Sea salt (.25 tsp.)
- Paprika (.5 tsp.)
- Pepper (.5 tsp.)
- Eggs (4)
- Cheddar cheese – shredded used (4 oz./110 g)
- Also Needed: Ramekins (4)

Prep Method:

1. Preheat the Air Fryer to 356° Fahrenheit/180° Celsius.
2. Grate the zucchini. Add the margarine to the ramekins and layer the zucchini in a nest shape. Sprinkle it using pepper, salt, and paprika.
3. Whisk the eggs - add to the nest, topping it off with the cheese.
4. Air-fry for seven minutes. Chill for three minutes and serve in the ramekin.

Chapter 2: Tasty Smoothies

You will be pleased to know that most smoothies can be refrigerated for one day or stored in the freezer for about three months. Frozen fruit can be safely defrosted in the refrigerator, but it can take up to six hours. Frozen fruit can be swiftly thawed in the microwave or fast defrosted in less than two hours by soaking it in cold water.

Make a Freezer Smoothie Pack

Servings: 5
Time Required: 15 minutes

Essential Ingredients:

- Fruit: Whole raspberries, blueberries, strawberries, or chopped mango (2.5 cups total)
- Sliced banana (2.5 cups)
- Soymilk or vanilla-almond unsweetened milk (5 cups)

Prep Method:

1. Make the packages using ½ cup of the chosen fruit or berries and ½ cup of banana into five sealable baggies or plastic containers.

2. Then pop them into the freezer to use when desired.
3. When you are ready to use one, add a baggie full to a blender with a cup of chosen milk.
4. Pulse till it is velvety smooth.

Smoothies in a Bowl

Almond-Mango Smoothie

Servings: 1
Time Required: 10 minutes

Essential Ingredients:

- Frozen mango – chopped (.5 cup)
- Greek nonfat plain yogurt (.5 cup)
- Frozen banana (.25 cup sliced)
- Almond unsweetened milk – plain (.25 cup)
- Unsalted almonds – separated (5 tbsp.)
- Ground allspice (.125 or 1/8 tsp.)
- Honey (.5 tsp.)
- Raspberries (.25 cup)

Prep Method:

1. Load the blender with yogurt, mango, milk, banana, allspice, and almonds (3 tbsp.).
2. Blend till it's velvety and pour into a serving bowl.
3. Garnish the smoothie with the berries, honey, and the rest of the almonds to serve.

Berry Smoothie

Servings: 2
Time Required: 5-6 minutes

Essential Ingredients:

- Unsweetened almond milk (.5 cup/125 ml)
- Chopped strawberries (2 oz./50 g)
- Crushed ice (3 cups/750 ml)
- <u>Pea/vanilla protein powder </u>(.33 cup/40 g)
- Psyllium husk powder (.5 tsp.)
- Coconut oil (1 tbsp.)
- Liquid Stevia (5 – 10 drops)

Prep Method:

1. Put the ice cubes in a blender and allow them to sit till they are slightly melted (5 min.)
2. Toss in the remainder of the fixings and mix until it's light pink and creamy.
3. Pour it into a serving bowl and top it off using desired toppings.

Other Delicious Favorites

Banana-Strawberry Smoothie

Servings: 1
Time Required: 5-6 minutes

Essential Ingredients:

- Almond milk - unsweetened (1 cup)
- Unsweetened plain yogurt/unsweetened plain kefir (.5 cup)
- Stevia (2 packets)
- Banana (¼ of 1 small)
- Fresh or frozen strawberries (.5 cup)
- Paleo Fiber powder/ground flaxseed meal/chia seed (1 tbsp.)
- Collagen hydrolysate/vanilla protein powder of your choice (1 tbsp.)
- Vanilla extract (.5 tsp.)

Prep Method:

1. Toss all the fixings into a blender.
2. Mix using the high-speed setting.

Carrot Smoothie

Servings: 3
Time Required: 35 minutes

Essential Ingredients:

- Carrots – sliced (1 cup)
- Orange peel – zested finely (.5 tsp.)
- Orange juice (1 cup)
- Ice cubes (1.5 cups)
- Orange peel curls (3 @ 1-inch each)

Prep Method:

1. Peel and slice the carrots. Then toss them into a covered saucepan with water till tender.
2. Drain, cool, and add them to the blender - mix.
3. Add the cubed ice and pulse till it is creamy as desired.
4. Serve in chilled glasses with a carrot curl.

Delicious Coffee & Oats Smoothie

Time Required: 12-15 minutes - varied

Essential Ingredients:

- Instant coffee granules (2 tsp. or to taste)
- Rolled oats (1 cup)
- Bananas (2)
- Milk of choice (2.5 cups)
- Chia seeds (1.5 tbsp.)
- Liquid stevia or another sweetener (2-3 drops/as desired)
- Optional: Cubed ice

Prep Method:

1. This is super easy since you can combine the chia seeds with oats and milk to soak (10 min. to overnight).
2. When ready, just toss all the fixings into the mixer to combine till it is velvety smooth.

Extra Green Smoothie – Option One

Servings: 1
Time Required: 5 minutes

Essential Ingredients:

- Large ripe banana (1)
- Baby kale (1 cup – packed)
- Almond milk - unsweetened – vanilla used (1 cup)
- Avocado (1/4 of 1 ripe)
- Chia seeds (1 tbsp.)
- Honey (2 tsp.)
- Ice cubes (1 cup)

Prep Method:

1. Toss each of the fixings into a blender.
2. Mix using the high setting till it's velvety smooth.
3. Add the cubes of ice and mix again to serve.

Extra-Green Avocado Smoothie – Option Two

Servings: 2
Time Required: 15 minutes

Essential Ingredients:

- Coconut/almond unsweetened milk (1.25 cups – chilled)
- Ripened banana and avocado (1 of each)
- Sliced sweet apple – Honeycrisp used (1)
- Celery stalk (1 small - chopped)
- Spinach or kale (2 cups – lightly packed)
- Fresh ginger (1-inch piece)
- Cubed ice (8)

Prep Method:

1. First, rinse and prepare the veggies for the smoothie.
2. Once in the blender, pulse till it is creamy and smooth.

Grapefruit-Pineapple Detox Smoothie

Servings: 2
Time Required: 10 minutes

Essential Ingredients:

- Coconut water – plain (1 cup)
- Pineapple – frozen & diced (1 cup)
- Baby spinach (1 cup – packed tightly)
- Small grapefruit (1)
- Freshly grated ginger (.5 tsp.)
- Ice (1 cup)

Prep Method:

1. First, do the prep as needed. You will need to peel and segment the grapefruit, while removing all the juice from the membranes.
2. Toss all the goodies prepared into the blender, mixing till frothy and smooth.

Green Tea Fruit Smoothie

Servings: 2
Time Required: 10 minutes

Essential Ingredients:

- Mixed fruit – pineapple & peaches used – frozen – unsweetened (2 cups)
- Honey (1 tbsp.)
- Green tea – unsweetened & chilled (1 cup)
- Lemon juice (1 tbsp.)

Prep Method:

1. Once the tea is chilled, add it with the rest of the fixings in your blender.
2. Pulse till it is creamy, and serve promptly.

Mango-Raspberry Smoothie

Servings: 1
Time Required: 5 minutes

Essential Ingredients:

- Water (.5 cup)
- Medium avocado (1)
- Lemon juice (1 tbsp.)
- Frozen mango (.75 cup)
- Frozen raspberries (.25 cup)
- Optional: Agave (1 tbsp.)

Prep Method:

1. Add and mix all the fixings in your blender.
2. Pulse till it is creamy to serve.

Minty Berry Kefir Smoothie

Servings: 2
Time Required: 5 minutes

Essential Ingredients:

- Plain low-fat kefir (1 cup – found in the dairy section)
- Frozen mixed berries (1 cup)
- Orange juice (.25 cup)
- Fresh mint (1-2 tbsp.)
- Honey (1 tbsp.)

Prep Method:

1. Measure and add all the fixings to your blender.
2. Process the mixture till it is creamy to serve.

Oatmeal Breakfast Smoothie

Servings: 2
Time Required: 4-5 minutes

Essential Ingredients:

- Uncooked-ground oats (1 cup)
- Frozen banana (2)
- Skim milk (3 cups)
- Ground flaxseeds (2 tbsp.)

Optional:
- Sugar substitute
- Instant coffee (2 tsp.)
- Also Needed: Spice/coffee grinder or food processor

Prep Method:

1. First, grind the oats and chop the banana into small bits before adding them to the machine.
2. Then serve it when ready.

Peanut Butter – Chocolate & Banana Smoothie

Servings: 2
Time Required: 5 minutes

Essential Ingredients:

- Nonfat milk (1 cup)
- Banana (1 frozen - medium)
- Peanut butter – natural-organic type (2 tbsp.)
- Cocoa powder - unsweetened (1 tbsp.)
- Hemp or chia seeds (1 tbsp. if desired)
- Vanilla extract (1 tsp.)

Prep Method:

1. Add each of the fixings to your blender and pulse till it is velvety smooth to serve.

Pineapple-Strawberry Smoothie

Servings: 1
Time Required: 5 minutes

Essential Ingredients:

- Strawberries - frozen (1 cup)
- Freshly chopped pineapple (1 cup)
- Chilled almond milk – unsweetened (.75 cup + more if needed)
- Almond butter (1 tbsp.)

Prep Method:

1. Toss the pineapple, strawberries, almond butter, and almond milk into a blender.
2. Pulse until it's creamy smooth, adding more almond milk, if needed, for desired consistency.
3. Serve immediately for the most flavorful result.

Strawberry Smoothie

Servings: 1
Time Required: 5 minutes

Essential Ingredients:

- Strawberries (5 medium)
- Unsweetened almond/soy milk (1 cup)
- Greek-style yogurt - L.F. (.5 cup)
- Ice (6 cubes)

Prep Method:

1. Toss each of the components into a blender, mixing until velvety.
2. Serve in a chilled glass with a fresh strawberry!

Vegan Avocado-Chocolate Smoothie

Servings: 2
Time Required: 5-6 minutes

Essential Ingredients:

- Ripe avocado (half of 1)
- Cocoa powder (3 tbsp.)
- Coconut milk - full-fat (1 cup)
- Water (.5 cup/1.2 dl)
- Lime juice (1 tsp.)
- Mineral salt (1 pinch)
- Liquid Stevia (6-7 drops)
- To Garnish: Fresh mint (as desired)

Prep Method:

1. Prepare and add all the measured fixings into the blender.
2. Mix using the high-speed setting until it's mixed and creamy. If desired, add more liquid stevia to taste.
3. Top it off using a sprig of fresh mint and serve.

Chapter 3: Fruity & Nut Favorites

Almond-Stuffed Dates

Servings: 1
Time Required: 5 minutes

Essential Ingredients:

- Salted whole almonds (2)
- Pitted Medjool pitted dates (2)
- Orange zest (.25 tsp.)

Prep Method:

1. Stuff each of the dates with one of the almonds.
2. Prepare the zest and roll each of the prepared dates through the mixture.
3. Enjoy as a snack anytime.
4. Note: Dates are rich in micronutrients that may also have benefits for diabetes and insulin resistance.

Berry Crumble

Servings: 1
Time Required: 20 minutes

Essential Ingredients:

- Fresh or frozen raspberries/mixed berries (1 cup/125 g)
- Stevia (1 tsp.)
- Vanilla protein powder (1 scoop)
- Oats (.25 cup/20g)
- Lemon juice (2 tbsp.)
- Almonds (10)
- Also Needed: Small Pyrex oven dish

Prep Method:

1. Preheat the oven to 350° Fahrenheit or 177 ° Celsius.
2. Toss the berries into the oven dish and dust with the Stevia over the top.
3. Combine the protein powder with oats and lemon juice. Chop the almonds into small pieces and mix them with the crumble.
4. Spread the crumble over the berries to bake (15 min.) Then, adjust the temperature to broil and continue baking the crumble for another one to two minutes until the top is browned to your liking.

5. Place the pan on the countertop to cool slightly before serving.

Chili-Lime Grilled Pineapple

Servings: 6
Time Required: 15 minutes

Essential Ingredients:

- Fresh pineapple (1)
- Lime juice (1 tbsp.)
- Olive oil (1 tbsp.)
- Honey or agave nectar/your preference (1 tbsp.)
- Brown sugar – or equivalent alternative (3 tbsp.)
- Chili powder (1.5 tsp.)
- Salt (1 dash)

Prep Method:

1. Peel the pineapple, removing any eyes from the fruit. Cut lengthwise into six wedges; remove the core. Mix the rest of the fixings until blended in a mixing container.
2. Brush the pineapple with half of the glaze; reserve the remaining mixture for basting.
3. Cover and grill the pineapple using the medium-temperature setting till lightly browned – basting occasionally using the reserved glaze (4 min. on each side).

Flavorful Marinated Oranges

Servings: 3-4
Time Required: 15 minutes (+) marinating time

Essential Ingredients:

- Orange juice (1 cup)
- Zested orange (1 tbsp.)
- Vanilla extract (1 tsp.)
- Lemon juice (1 tbsp.)
- Zested lemon (1 tsp.)
- Sugar (1 tbsp.)
- Medium oranges (4/about 3 cups)
- Optional: Lime zest strips & vanilla yogurt

Prep Method:

1. Mix the fixings up to the line (***), mixing till the sugar has liquified.
2. Peel & thinly slice the oranges. Add them to a glass bowl and add the juice mixture.
3. Refrigerate, covered, until flavors are blended (2-3 hrs.). If desired, top with lime zest strips and serve with yogurt.

Maple Apples

Servings: 5 @ ½ apple each
Time Required: 21-25 minutes

Essential Ingredients:

- Tart apple – Granny Smith used (2)
- Juiced lemon (1 tbsp.)
- Canola oil (1 tsp.)
- Maple syrup – sugar-free (1 tbsp.)
- Apple cider (.25 cup)
- Ground cloves & cinnamon (.25 tsp. each)
- For Serving: Toasted & slivered almonds (1 tbsp.)

Prep Method:

1. Slice but do not peel the apple into ½-inch wedges, tossing them into the lemon juice.
2. Prepare a big fry pan to warm the oil (medium temperature).
3. Now, toss in the apples to sauté (3 min.).
4. Modify the heat to low, put a lid on the pan, and simmer while stirring occasionally (6-7 min.).
5. Transfer the apples from the pan and set aside.
6. Now toss in the rest of the fixings (omit the almonds for now).

7. Simmer using a med-high temperature setting till it is syrupy.
8. Now combine all the goodies, dust with the almonds, and serve.

Mini Apple Chimichanga

Servings: 4
Time Required: 30 minutes

Essential Ingredients:

- Apple (2)
- Granulated sweetener favorite/Splenda or another 0-cal (3 tbsp,)
- Ground cinnamon (.5 tsp.)
- Water (.25 cup)
- Whole wheat flour tortillas – 8-inch (4)
- Nonstick cooking spray (as needed)

Prep Method:

1. Set the oven to 400° Fahrenheit/204° Celsius.
2. Remove the core and chop the apples.
3. Use a medium-sized saucepan and toss in the fixings (apples, 2 tbsp. Splenda, water, and cinnamon. Simmer till the apples are softened. Place the pan onto a cool burner and wait until it is room temperature.
4. Make the chimichangas, add the apple filling (2 tsp.) on each tortilla and fold each end over the filling.
5. Next, roll the tortillas up and secure each one with a toothpick. Lightly coat the tortillas with cooking spray.

6. Arrange the folded tortillas seam-side facing downward on the baking tray.
7. Sprinkle evenly with the remaining granulated sweetener.
8. Bake for five minutes, flip, and continue baking (5 min.).
9. Transfer the chimichangas from the baking sheet and place them on individual plates to serve as desired.

Picnic Berry Shortcakes

Servings: 4
Time Required: 20-25 minutes (+) chilling time

Essential Ingredients:

- Water (2 tbsp.)
- Sugar (2 tbsp.)
- Cornstarch (.5 tsp.)
- Fresh strawberries - divided (2 cups)
- Grated lime zest (.5 tsp.)
- Fresh blueberries (2 cups)
- Round sponge cakes (2 - individually sized)
- Optional: Whipped topping
- Also Needed: Wide-mouth half-pint canning jars (4)

Prep Method:

1. Use a saucepan to combine the cornstarch with the sugar. Pour in the water. Slice and add one cup of the strawberries and mash the mixture.
2. Once boiling - simmer - stirring until thickened (1-2 min.).
3. Now, move the pan to a cool spot, and mix in lime zest. Pour it into a small container and pop it into the fridge, covered until chilled.

4. Slice the sponge cakes crosswise into halves. Trim them to fit in the bottoms of the jars.
5. Toss the blueberries and the rest of the strawberries over the cakes. Pour the sauce over the tops and garnish to your liking.

Warm & Spicy Apples

Servings: 6
Time Required: 20 minutes

Essential Ingredients:

- Red-skinned cooking apples - ex. Jonathon or Rome (5 medium/about 7 cups)
- Water (.25 cup)
- Cinnamon (.5 tsp.)
- Ground nutmeg (.125 tsp./as desired)
- Honey (2 tbsp.)

Prep Method:

1. Remove the core, quarter, and thinly slice the apples.
2. Combine the sliced apples with the water in a big skillet. Sprinkle with nutmeg and cinnamon. Once boiling, lower the temperature setting.
3. Put a top on the pot and simmer until the apples are just tender, stirring once or twice (3 min.).
4. Drizzle with honey and toss to coat.
5. Serve warm in six individual serving bowls.

Nuts & Berries with Whipped Cheese

Servings: 4
Time Required: 5-10 minutes

Essential Ingredients:

- Sugar-free maple syrup (2 tbsp./30 ml)
- Low-fat no-salt added cottage cheese (2 cups/500 ml.)
- Fresh blackberries (2 cups)
- Unsalted shelled pistachios - coarsely chopped (.5 cup/125 ml.)
- Also Needed: Food processor or blender

Prep Method:

1. Toss the syrup and cottage cheese into a blender
2. Use the high setting to pulse for one minute.
3. Add the rest of the fixings to the dish and serve.

Part 2: Air Fryer Meal Favorites

Since you have such a busy schedule, the Air Fryer can be your best friend!

Chapter 4: Chicken Time

Breast of Chicken

Servings: 4
Required Time: 25 minutes

Essential Ingredients:

- Chicken breast (1 lb. or 450 g)
- Olive oil (1 tsp.)
- Pepper (.5 tsp.)
- Salt (1 tsp.)
- As Desired: Spices & herbs

Prep Method:

1. Place the chicken on the countertop for 20-30 minutes before cooking time. Trim it to remove all fat and bones.
2. When you're ready to cook, warm the Air Fryer unit to reach 360° Fahrenheit/182° Celsius.
3. Pat the chicken dry using several paper towels.

4. Drizzle with oil, then dust it with the desired spices.
5. Place the chicken in the tray and insert it into the fryer.
6. Set the timer for 20 minutes. When ready, remove from the tray.
7. Wait about five minutes before serving.

Chicken Meatballs

Servings: 16 balls
Time Required: 20 minutes

Essential Ingredients:

- Zucchini (1 large)
- Ground chicken (1 lb./450 g)
- Garlic powder (1 tbsp.)
- Dried oregano (.5 tbsp.)
- Red pepper flakes (.5 tbsp.)
- Fresh parsley (2 tbsp.)
- Egg (1)
- Pepper - divided (.5 tbsp./ to taste)
- Salt (as desired)

Prep Method:

1. Warm the Air Fryer to reach 400° Fahrenheit/204° Celsius.
2. Finely grate the zucchini into a mesh strainer. Add salt (½ tbsp.) to extract the excess water - placing it over the sink while you prep the other ingredients.
3. Gently press the grated zucchini to drain the excess liquid.
4. Chop the parsley. Add the ground chicken, garlic powder, red pepper flakes, parsley, oregano, egg, and drained zucchini to a mixing container.

5. Prepare the mix into 16 one-inch balls (@ 1 tbsp. each).
6. Arrange the meatballs in the fryer with space between them (working in batches if needed for 10 to 12 min.), turning them once till they are done.

Chicken Nuggets

Servings: 8
Required Time: 30 minutes

Essential Ingredients:

- Buttermilk (1 cup)
- Eggs (2)
- Chicken tenderloins - cut into nugget size (2 lb./910 g)
- Flour (1 cup)
- Paprika (1 tbsp.)
- Parmesan cheese - grated (3 tbsp.)
- Salt & pepper (1 tsp. each)
- Parsley flakes (1 tbsp.)
- Panko breadcrumbs (2 cups)
- Cooking spray (as needed)

Prep Method:

1. Mix the buttermilk and chicken in a big mixing container for a few minutes to soak while preparing the seasoned flour.
2. Whisk the flour with paprika, pepper, parmesan, parsley, and salt in a mixing container. Fully beat the eggs in another dish.
3. Pour the breadcrumbs onto a flat plate.
4. Dredge each nugget in flour, eggs, and breadcrumbs.
5. Preheat the Air Fryer to 400° Fahrenheit/204° Celsius.

6. Spray the basket using a cooking oil spray. Put as many nuggets into the basket as you can without overcrowding.
7. Spritz the tops using a little cooking oil spray.
8. Air-fry for ten minutes, flip, and continue cooking (2 min.)
9. Remove and repeat the process with the remaining nuggets.

Chicken Thighs

Servings: 8 or 4.5 cups shredded
Time Required: 16-20 minutes

Essential Ingredients:

- Chicken thighs (2 lb. or 910 g)
- Avocado oil or another oil (2 tsp.)
- Chili powder (2 tsp.)
- Pepper (.5 tsp.)
- Cumin (1 tsp.)
- Cayenne pepper (1 pinch)
- Garlic powder (1 tsp.)
- Salt (1 tsp.)

Prep Method:

1. Warm the fryer unit to reach 400° Fahrenheit/204° Celsius.
2. Combine the garlic and chili powder, pepper, cumin, salt, and cayenne.
3. Trim the chicken - removing all skin and bones - dabbing it dry using several paper towels, rub with oil, and sprinkle evenly on both sides with spice mixture.
4. Place chicken in the fryer basket and cook until chicken registers 175° Fahrenheit/79° Celsius (12-16 min.).
5. Flip halfway through cooking, if desired.
6. Slightly cool the chicken and shred or chop into small chunks.
7. Serve the chicken with lime wedges over salad or in tortillas with taco toppings.

Crispy Cornish Hen

Servings: 3
Time Required: 30 minutes

Essential Ingredients:

- Cornish hen (1)
- Black pepper & salt (to your liking)
- Paprika (to taste)
- Coconut/olive oil cooking spray

Prep Method:

1. Set the fryer unit at 390° Fahrenheit/199° Celsius.
2. Rub the hen with spices.
3. Spray the Air fryer basket with the oil spray.
4. Arrange the hen in the Air fryer for 25 minutes. Turn halfway through the cooking cycle.
5. Carefully remove and serve.

Crumbly Tenderloin of Chicken

Servings: 4
Time Required: 30 minutes

Essential Ingredients:
- Egg (1)
- Dry breadcrumbs (.5 cup)
- Vegetable oil (2 tbsp.)
- Chicken (8 tenderloins)

Prep Method:
1. Warm the Air Fryer to 350° Fahrenheit/177° Celsius.
2. Whisk the egg in a mixing container.
3. Toss the breadcrumbs with the oil in a second bowl till it's crumbly.
4. Dip the pieces of chicken into the egg dish, shaking off any residual egg.
5. Dredge chicken through the crumb mixture, making sure it's thoroughly covered.
6. Arrange the tenderloins into the Air Fryer basket. Cook until the centers are no longer pink (12 min.).
7. The chickens' center should read at least 165° Fahrenheit/74° Celsius when tested with a cooking thermometer.

Frozen Chicken Patties

Servings: 1
Time Required: 7-8 minutes

Essential Ingredients:

- Burger buns (2)
- Chicken patties – fully frozen (2)

Prep Method:
1. Heat the Air Fryer at 400° Fahrenheit/204° Celsius.
2. Place the poultry in the unit, flipping once during the cooking cycle (7-9 min.)
3. If adding cheese, turn the fryer off. Then place the patty on the bun and close the unit to air fry till the cheese is melted to your liking (30-60 sec.). Then extinguish the heat.
4. When ready, top as desired.

Jamaican Fajitas

Servings: 4
Time Required: 25 minutes

Essential Ingredients:
- Breast of chicken (2)
- Bell peppers (2)
- Red onion (.25 cup)
- Lime (1)
- Taco seasoning/your preference (1 tsp.)
- Olive oil (1 tbsp.)
- Pepper & salt (as desired)
- To Serve: Lime/cilantro juice

Prep Method:

1. Preheat the Air Fryer to 390° Fahrenheit or 199° Celsius.
2. Prepare the fixings by slicing the chicken, onion, and peppers.
3. Toss the fixings thoroughly and arrange in the fryer basket.
4. Wait for them to air fry till done or 165° Fahrenheit or 74° Celsius – internal temp (15 min.)
5. Serve it as desired.

Lemon Pepper Chicken Breast

Servings: 3
Time Required: 23-25 minutes

Essential Ingredients:

- Chicken breasts (3 large)
- Black pepper (2 tsp.)
- Garlic powder (1 tsp.)
- Sea salt (.5 tsp.)
- Lemon (1 medium)

Prep Method:

1. Set the Air Fryer at 360° Fahrenheit or 182° Celsius.
2. Rinse and place the chicken on a chopping block.
3. Drizzle them with the rind and juice of lemon with a sprinkle of salt, garlic powder, and pepper.
4. Put the chicken into the fryer basket. Slice lemons and arrange them to surround the chicken.
5. Check the chicken and then cook for an additional three to five minutes if they are still pink in the middle.
6. Slice the chicken breasts and serve.

Southwestern-Style Chicken Fajitas

Servings: 4
Time Required: 28-30 minutes

Essential Ingredients:

- Chicken breast (1 lb. or 450 g)
- Olive oil (2 tsp.)
- Bell peppers (2)
- Onion (1)
- Salt (1 tsp.)
- Cayenne (1 pinch)
- Chili powder (2 tsp.)
- Pepper (.5 tsp.)
- Cumin (1 tsp.)

Prep Method:

1. Set the Air Fryer unit to reach 360° Fahrenheit/182° Celsius.
2. Trim the chicken to remove all fat and bones - slice it. Slice the onion and peppers.
3. Toss the veggies and prepared chicken into a mixing container. Mix in the oil, salt, cayenne, chili powder, pepper, and cumin.
4. Toss to mix and dump the mix into the Air Fryer tray.

5. Air-fry for 16 to 20 minutes. Check it at the halfway marker (10 min.) Stir the fixings until the mixture is combined.
6. After the fajitas are browned as desired, enjoy them served in a salad, tortillas, or over a delicious bed of rice with desired toppings.

Sweet Chili Wings

Servings: 4
Required Time: 25 minutes

Essential Ingredients:
- Chicken wing portions (1 lb.)
- Flour – all-purpose used (0.5 cup)
- To Garnish: Cilantro or green onion

    For the Sauce:
- Sweet chili sauce/or another sauce (1 cup)
- Lime - juiced (1)
- Ginger (.5 tsp.)
- Garlic clove (1)
- Sriracha/red pepper flakes (.5 tsp.)
- As Needed: Cooking oil spray

Prep Method:
1. Heat the Air Fryer at 400° Fahrenheit/204° Celsius. Spritz the fryer basket with a bit of spray.
2. Prepare the chicken into flats, drumettes, and wing portions. Use a bunch of paper towels to dry the chicken wings.
3. Then toss them into a mixing container with flour.
4. Arrange the chicken in the prepared fryer to cook (8 min.).
5. Flip the wings over and continue cooking (approx. 8 min.).

6. Meanwhile, mince the garlic and toss the sauce fixings in a big mixing container.
7. And the prepared wings in the sauce and place them back in the fryer – single-layered to cook (2 min.).
8. Garnish as desired and serve.

Turkey Meatballs

Servings: 4
Time Required: 15 minutes

Essential Ingredients:

- Turkey mince (1.5 lb./675 g)
- Red bell pepper (1 deseeded & finely chopped)
- Egg (1 large)
- Minced fresh herbs - ex. - parsley (4 tbsp.)
- Minced fresh cilantro coriander (1 tbsp.)
- Salt & black pepper (as desired)

Prep Method:

1. Warm the Air Fryer to 400° Fahrenheit/204° Celsius.
2. Whisk the egg to combine it with the rest of the ingredients.
3. Shape into meatballs - about 1¼-inches each.
4. Put half the meatballs in a single layer in the fryer basket.
5. Air-fry for seven to ten minutes till they're lightly browned as desired (shaking halfway through).
6. Remove and keep warm and continue with the rest of the meatballs.
7. Serve warm with toothpicks and a dipping sauce for a snack or as a meal.

Veggies & Chicken

Servings: 4
Time Required: 20 minutes

Essential Ingredients:

- Chicken breast (1 lb./2-3 medium/450 g)
- Broccoli florets - fresh or frozen (1 cup)
- Zucchini (1)
- Bell pepper (1 cup)
- Onion (half of 1)
- Garlic (2 cloves)
- Olive oil (2 tbsp.)
- Italian seasoning or spice blend of choice (1 tbsp.)
- Garlic powder - chili powder (.5 tsp. each)
- Black pepper & salt (.5 tsp. each/as desired)

Prep Method:

1. Warm the Air Fryer to 400° Fahrenheit/204° Celsius.
2. If your air fryer is small, you may have to cook them in two to three batches.
3. Mince the garlic. Dice the veggies and chicken into small-size chunks and toss them into a big mixing container. Add

the oil and seasoning - toss thoroughly to mix.
4. Arrange the chicken and veggies in the fryer. Air-fry them for ten minutes, shaking halfway through the cycle. Serve as desired.

Chapter 5: Pork Time

Broccoli & Chops

Servings: 2
Time Required: 10-15 minutes

Essential Ingredients:

- Bone-in pork chops (2 @ 5 oz./140 g each)
- Avocado oil, divided (2 tbsp.)
- Onion & Garlic powder (.5 tsp. each)
- Salt - divided (1 tsp.)
- Paprika (.5 tsp.)
- Broccoli florets (2 cups)
- Garlic (2 cloves - minced)

Prep Method:

1. Warm the Air Fryer to 350° Fahrenheit/177° Celsius.
2. Spray the basket using a non-stick cooking oil spray.
3. Drizzle oil (1 tbsp.) on both sides of the chops and season using paprika, onion powder, garlic powder, and salt (½ tsp.).
4. Place the pork chops in the fryer basket to air-fry (5 min.).
5. Meanwhile, toss the broccoli, garlic, remainder of the salt (½ tsp.), and

remaining tablespoon of oil into a mixing container - toss to coat.
6. Carefully turn the chops. Add the broccoli to the basket and return to the fryer.
7. Air-fry for five more minutes, stirring the broccoli halfway through. Carefully remove to serve.

Pork Bites

Servings: 4
Time Required: 16-20 minutes

Essential Ingredients:

- Cajun seasoning (1 tbsp.)
- Pork tenderloins (1 lb.)
- Olive oil (2 tbsp.)

Prep Method:

1. Warm the fryer at 400° Fahrenheit/204° Celsius.
2. Evenly cut the pork into bite-sized bits.
3. Toss the meat with seasoning and oil in a mixing container.
4. Arrange them in a single layer in the basket.
5. Set the time for five to six minutes till the pork's internal temperature reaches 145° Fahrenheit/63° Celsius.

Pork Chops – Breaded

Servings: 6
Time Required: 28-30 minutes

Essential Ingredients:

- Pork chops (3 @ 6 oz.)
- Breadcrumbs (.5 cups)
- Egg (1 large)
- Cooking oil spray (as needed)

For Spices:
- Black pepper & salt
- Smoked paprika
- Garlic powder

Prep Method:

1. For this recipe, it is important to preheat the fryer for four minutes at 380° Fahrenheit/194 ° Celsius.
2. Fully rinse and dab dry the pork.
3. First, whisk an egg for the first dish. Then combine the garlic powder with the paprika, pepper, and salt to dust the meat. Roll the chops through the breadcrumbs.
4. Lightly mist the pork with spray to coat and air fry (8-12 min.).
5. Flip them over and continue till browned and have reached an internal temperature of

6. The pork chops should be cooked for a further six minutes after flipping them, or until browned and the internal temperature reaches 145° Fahrenheit/160 ° Celsius. Serve while they are piping hot.

Pork Chops – Ranch-Style

Servings: 4
Time Required: 15 minutes

Essential Ingredients:

- Pork chops (4 boneless)
- Oil (2 tsp.)
- Ranch seasoning mix (1 tbsp. - see recipe Ch. 7/or preferred option)
- Salt & pepper (as desired)
- To Garnish: Chopped parsley

Prep Method:

1. Warm the Air Fryer unit to 380° Fahrenheit/194° Celsius.
2. Pat pork chops dry with a paper towel. Drizzle the oil over both sides of each pork chop, and spread to coat evenly. Sprinkle the fresh seasoning mix evenly over the chops and dust using a bit of pepper and salt.
3. Air fry the pork until the internal temperature of pork chops reaches 145° Fahrenheit/63° Celsius - flipping at the halfway marker (10 min.).
4. Garnish cooked pork chops with fresh chopped parsley, if desired.

Pork Steaks

Servings: 2
Time Required: 8-10 minutes

Essential Ingredients:

- Pork steaks (2)
- Pepper & salt (as desired)

Prep Method:

1. Set the unit at 360° Fahrenheit/182° Celsius.
2. Arrange the steaks in the basket of the Air Fryer - not touching.
3. Season to your liking with salt and pepper. Close the fryer.
4. Air-fry for eight minutes to serve.

Chapter 6: Seafood Time

Shrimp Favorites

Air-Fried Dragon Shrimp

Servings: 2
Time Required: 20 minutes

Essential Ingredients:

- Almond flour (.25 cup)
- Ginger (1 pinch)
- Chopped onions (1 cup)
- Shrimp (.5 lb.)
- Eggs (2)
- Soya sauce (.5 cup)
- Olive oil (2 tbsp.)

Prep Method:

1. Warm the Air Fryer until it reaches 390° Fahrenheit.
2. Boil the shrimp for about five minutes.
3. Make a paste from the mixture of smashed onions and ginger.
4. Whisk the eggs with the remainder of the ingredients and toss the shrimp into the mixture.
5. Add to the fryer for 10 minutes to serve.

Breaded Fried Shrimp

Servings: 4
Time Required: 10 minutes

Essential Ingredients:

- Egg white (3 tbsp. or 1 egg)
- Raw shrimp (1 lb.)
- Flour – all-purpose used (.5 cup)
- Breadcrumbs – Panko suggested (.75 cup)
- Paprika (1 tsp.)
- Pepper and salt to your liking
- Montreal Chicken Seasoning of choice
- Cooking oil spray

The Sauce:
- Sriracha (2 tbsp.)
- Plain non-fat Greek yogurt (.33 cup)
- Sweet chili sauce (.25 cup)

Prep Method:

1. Peel and devein the shrimp.
2. Warm up the Air Fryer to 400° Fahrenheit.
3. Add the seasonings to the shrimp.
4. Use three bowls for the breadcrumbs, egg whites, and flour.
5. Scoot the shrimp around in the flour, egg, and, lastly, the breadcrumbs.
6. Lightly spray the shrimp and add it to

the fryer basket for four minutes. Flip the shrimp over and cook for another four minutes. Watch the last few minutes to prevent burning.
7. *For the Sauce*: Combine all the fixings and mix thoroughly.

Chinese-Cuisine Garlic Prawns

Servings: 4
Time Required: 20-25 minutes

Essential Ingredients:
- Butter - unsalted (5 tbsp.)
- Olive oil (2 tbsp.)
- Raw shrimp - jumbo (1 lb. or 453.5 g)
- Minced garlic (2 tsp.)
- Salt (.5 tsp.)
- Pepper (.25 tsp.)
- To Garnish: Fresh parsley

Prep Method:
1. Set the fryer unit at 390° Fahrenheit/199° Celsius.
2. First, melt the butter. Mince/dice the parsley and garlic.
3. Toss the fixings in a big mixing container – then smother the shrimp.
4. Air fry till done to your liking (8-10 min.). Garnish as desired to serve.

Coconut Shrimp

Servings: 4 or 6 shrimp @ 4 oz./110 g portion
Time Required: 20 minutes

Essential Ingredients:

- Jumbo raw shrimp (1 lb./450 g or 20-30)
- Egg whites (2)
- Water (1 tbsp.)
- Whole-wheat panko breadcrumbs (.5 cup)
- Turmeric (.5 tsp.)
- Unsweetened coconut flakes (.25 cup)
- Ground cumin & coriander (.5 tsp. each)
- Salt (.125 or 1/8 tsp.)

Prep Method:

1. Set the temperature of the Air Fryer unit to 400° Fahrenheit/204° Celsius.
2. Peel and remove the veins from the shrimp - dry them using several paper towels. Whisk the egg whites and water in a shallow mixing container.
3. Combine the panko breadcrumbs, coconut, cumin, turmeric, coriander, and salt in another shallow mixing container.
4. Dip the shrimp in the egg mixture - coat in the panko mix.

5. Arrange the coated shrimp on a wire rack. Repeat with all shrimp.
6. Arrange the shrimp - single-layered in the fryer basket. Spray the shrimp with nonstick cooking spray for two seconds - air fry for four minutes.
7. Flip the shrimp - air-fry till the shrimp are golden brown (2-4 min.). Serve warm.

Other Seafood Options

Basil & Tomato Scallops

Servings: 2
Time Required: 15-20 minutes

Essential Ingredients:

- Jumbo sea scallops (8)
- Frozen spinach (12 oz.)
- Vegetable oil to spray (as needed)
- Tomato paste (1 tbsp.)
- Heavy whipping cream (.75 cup)
- Fresh basil (1 tbsp.)
- Garlic (1 tsp.)
- Pepper & salt (.5 tsp. each)
- Additional salt and pepper - to season scallops
- *Also Needed:* 7-inch heat-proof pan

Prep Method:

1. Thaw and drain the spinach. Mince the garlic and basil.
2. Spray the pan. Scoop a layer of spinach into the pan.
3. Mist the scallops with oil. Dust with pepper and salt and scatter them over the spinach.
4. Combine the basil, garlic, cream, tomato paste, salt, and pepper, adding it to the spinach and scallops.

5. Set the Air Fryer at 350° Fahrenheit for 10 minutes to cook until the scallops are cooked thoroughly. The sauce will also be bubbling.
6. Serve immediately.

Dungeness Crab Legs - Fresh or Frozen

Servings: 2
Time Required: 6-7 minutes

Essential Ingredients:

- Crab legs (1 lb.) or Crab leg clusters (2)
- Cajun seasoning (1 tsp.)
- Butter - melted for dipping (.5 cup)

Prep Method:

1. Season crab legs with the old bay or Cajun spices and place them in the air fryer.
2. Air-Fry for five minutes at 345° Fahrenheit/174° Celsius (no need to preheat).
3. Crack the legs and dip the crab meat in butter for extra flavor as desired.

Fried Rice & Sriracha Salmon

Servings: 4
Required Time: 25 minutes

Essential Ingredients:

- Cooked rice (2 cups)
- Mixed vegetables (12 oz./340 g bag - frozen)
- Soy sauce - divided (3 tsp.)
- Garlic & onion powder (.5 tsp. each)
- Pepper (.5 tsp.)
- Sriracha (1 tbsp.)
- Salmon fillet (1 lb./450 g)
- Honey (1 tsp.)
- Lime (half of 1 - juiced)

Prep Method:

1. Set the Air Fryer to 360° Fahrenheit/182° Celsius.
2. Pour the rice, mixed vegetables, soy sauce (2 tsp.), onion powder, pepper, and garlic powder into the fryer tray.
3. Air-fry for five to six minutes. Once the rice is crispy, scoop it into a bowl
4. Arrange the salmon in the Air Fryer tray.
5. Whisk the remainder of the soy sauce with lime juice, sriracha, and honey. Brush the mix over the salmon and place the tray back into the Air Fryer. Cook until the skin is crispy (15 min.).

6. Serve the delicious salmon over a portion of the hot rice.

Fried Salmon Cakes

Servings: 2
Time Required: 12 minutes

Essential Ingredients:

- Salmon fillet - fresh - frozen ok (8 oz./230 g)
- Eggs (1)
- Salt (.125 or 1/8 tsp.)
- Garlic powder (.25 tsp.)
- Sliced lemon (1)

Prep Method:

1. Mince the salmon and combine with a whisked egg and spices.
2. Shape the mixture into salmon cakes.
3. Set the Air Fryer temperature setting at 390° Fahrenheit/199° Celsius.
4. Slice and arrange the lemons in the fryer basket and add the salmon patties.
5. Air-fry for seven minutes.
6. Serve with your favorite diabetic-friendly sauce or dip.

Frozen Fish

Servings: 2
Time Required: 19-20 minutes

Essential Ingredients:

- Panko breadcrumbs (2 tbsp.)
- Garlic powder (.125 or 1/8 tsp.)
- Kosher salt (.25 tsp.)
- Olive oil spray (as needed)
- Tilapia filets (2 frozen)

Prep Method:

1. Set the Air Fryer unit to reach 370° Fahrenheit/188° Celsius.
2. Toss the breadcrumbs with salt and garlic powder.
3. Spritz or brush each fish filet with olive oil.
4. Spoon breadcrumbs (1 tbsp.) over each filet, spreading it evenly to coat the entire top of the filet. Press gently to help the breading adhere.
5. Then arrange the fish - breaded side up the fryer unit.
6. Air-fry until piping hot and browned as desired (12-14 min.).

Salmon Fillets

Servings: 2
Time Required: 20 minutes

Essential Ingredients:

- Salmon fillets (2 @ 4-6 oz. or 110-170 g each)
- Black pepper & salt (as desired)
- Lemon (1)
- Lemon juice (1 tsp.)
- Greek yogurt (.25 cup)
- Garlic powder (.5 tsp.)
- Fresh dill (1 tbsp.)

Prep Method:

1. Set the Air Fryer at 330° Fahrenheit/166° Celsius.
2. Fully wash – then dab the fillets dry with a few paper towels. Slice the lemon and cover the Air Fryer basket.
3. Dust the fillet using salt and pepper - arrange them over the lemons.
4. Air-fry for 15 minutes.
5. Chop the dill and make the sauce by combining the yogurt with dill, salt, pepper, and garlic powder. Drizzle using lemon juice as desired.
6. Once the salmon is done, cover it with sauce and serve.

Swordfish Kebabs

Servings: 2
Time Required: 20 minutes

Essential Ingredients:

- Swordfish steak (1)
- Zucchini (1)
- Bell pepper (1)
- Onion (1)
- Lemon (1)
- Skewers (2/as needed)
- Black pepper & salt (to taste)

Prep Method:

1. Set the Air Fryer at 375° Fahrenheit/191° Celsius.
2. Soak wooden skewers in the water for about ten minutes.
3. Meanwhile, slice the fish, zucchini, onions, and peppers into bite-size chunks.
4. Thread each of the fixings onto skewers – dusting with a portion of salt and pepper.
5. Slice the lemon into thin pieces and place it on the bottom of the fryer basket.
6. Add the kebabs on top of lemon slices. Air-fry for ten minutes to serve.

Chapter 7: Side Dish Favorites

Choose from any of these delicious dishes anytime.

Asparagus

Servings: 2
Time Required: 15-20 minutes

Essential Ingredients:

- Olive oil (1 tbsp.)
- Asparagus (1 lb. or 450 g)
- Garlic (1 clove)
- Pepper & salt (.125 or 1/8 tsp. each)

Prep Method:

1. Set the unit at 380° Fahrenheit/194° Celsius.
2. Trim the asparagus and trim the ends. Mince the garlic.
3. Place asparagus in a mixing container - add the remaining ingredients. Toss to combine.
4. Preheat the Air Fryer and add the asparagus - air-fry until tender (6 min.).

Bacon-Brussels Sprouts

Servings: 4
Required Time: 25-30 minutes

Essential Ingredients:

- Brussels sprouts (1 lb./450 g)
- Olive or avocado oil (.25 cup)
- Pure maple syrup (.25 cup)
- Vinegar - apple cider (1 tbsp.)
- Pepper (.25 tsp.)
- Salt (.5 tsp.)
- Bacon (4 @ ½-inch slices)

Prep Method:

1. Preheat the *oven* to 350° Fahrenheit or 177° Celsius.
2. Trim and halve the washed Brussels sprouts, removing discolored leaves. Larger sprouts may need to be quartered to keep sprouts uniform in size.
3. Whisk the oil with maple syrup, vinegar, pepper, and salt.
4. Fold the sprouts and raw bacon pieces into the bowl - gently stir to cover.
5. Spoon coated sprouts and bacon into the *air fryer*. (Note that any extra glaze/sauce will just fall to the bottom of the fryer.)
6. Air fry for 10-15 minutes until bacon and sprouts reach desired crispiness.

Halfway through cooking, open the drawer and stir contents.

Baked Potatoes with Broccoli & Cheese

Servings: 8
Time Required: 30 minutes

Essential Ingredients:

- Russet potatoes (4 medium @ 6-7 oz. or 170-200 g each)
- Milk - reduced-fat - divided (1 cup)
- A.P. flour (2 tbsp.)
- Shredded cheddar cheese - extra-sharp - divided (.5 cup)
- Broccoli florets (1 cup)
- Cayenne pepper (.25 tsp.)
- Kosher salt (.25 tsp.)
- To Garnish: Chives

Prep Method:

1. Warm the unit to 350° Fahrenheit/177° Celsius.
2. Pierce each of the potatoes using a fork. Put them onto a microwave-safe plate - to cook using the high setting (5 min.). Turn the potatoes - microwave another five minutes.
3. Warm a saucepan of milk (3/4 cup) - simmer using a medium-high heat setting.

4. Whisk the rest of the milk (1/4 cup) with flour in another mixing container till it's smooth.
5. Whisk the flour mixture into the pan till it's creamy and smooth. Wait for it to boil.
6. Transfer the pan from the burner and reserve two tablespoons of cheddar.
7. Stir the rest of the cheddar into the pan - mixing till it's smooth. Coarsely chop and stir in broccoli, cayenne, and salt.
8. Slice the potatoes into halves - gently mash the inside of each potato just until loose and crumbly.
9. Place four halves at a time in the basket of the fryer unit.
10. Top each with broccoli mixture (¼ cup) - divide one tablespoon of cheddar among the potatoes.
11. Air-fry the potatoes until the cheese is melted and the potato skins are crispy (5 min.).
12. Continue with the remaining broccoli mixture and cheddar over the potatoes.
13. Chop the chives and top the potatoes with them to serve.

Breaded Eggplant

Servings: 6
Time Required: 25-30 minutes

Essential Ingredients:

- Eggplant (1 medium - sliced ¼-inch rounds
- Flour – all-purpose is okay (.5 cup)
- Egg - beaten (1)
- Breadcrumbs – Panko used (2 cups)
- Italian seasoning (1.5 tbsp.)
- Pepper (.25 tsp.)
- Salt (.125 or 1/8 tsp.)
- Olive oil spray (as needed)

Prep Method:

1. Prepare three shallow bowls. Start by whisking the egg in one, put flour in another, and mix Panko breadcrumbs with seasonings in the third.
2. Warm the Air Fryer to 380° Fahrenheit/194° Celsius (5 min.). Lightly spray the fryer basket.
3. Slice the stem end off - discard. Slice it into ¼-inch rounds. Whisk the egg.
4. One at a time, dip into the flour, then into the egg, and press breadcrumbs on both sides till coated.
5. Put into the fryer basket, so they're not overlapping.

6. Cook for eight minutes, flip and spray the tops lightly.
7. Air-fry for another three minutes.

Breaded Mushrooms

Servings: 6
Time Required: 25 minutes

Essential Ingredients:

- Flour – all-purpose is okay (1 cup)
- Low-carb breadcrumbs (.5 cup)
- Seasonings (1.5 tsp.)
- Eggs (2)
- Water (.5 tbsp.)
- Mushrooms (1 lb./450 g)

Prep Method:

1. Lightly spray the Air Fryer basket and set it at 360° Fahrenheit/182° Celsius.
2. Rinse and drain the mushrooms.
3. Prepare two shallow dredging dishes.
4. Whisk the breadcrumbs, flour substitution, and seasonings.
5. In another container, whisk the water with the eggs.
6. Use a fork to dip the mushrooms in the egg bowl and into the flour mixture.
7. Arrange them in the basket - not touching. Prepare in batches as needed.
8. Air-fry for eight to ten minutes until nicely browned and crunchy to your liking.

Brussels Sprouts

Servings: 4
Required Time: 25 minutes

Essential Ingredients:

- Olive oil (1 tbsp.)
- Brussels sprouts (1 lb. or 450 g)
- Salt (.5 tsp. or as desired)
- Pepper (.25 tsp. or as desired)

Optional:
- Garlic powder (.5 tsp. or to your liking)
- Balsamic vinegar (1 tbsp.)

Prep Method:

1. Set the Air Fryer unit to heat at 360° Fahrenheit/182° Celsius.
2. Rinse the sprouts with water – pat them dry with a few paper towels.
3. Slice the bottom stem. Cut each of the sprouts into halves. Toss the sprouts in a mixing container with oil, garlic powder, pepper, balsamic vinegar, and salt. Scoop them into the fryer basket.
4. Air fry them until they're browned to your liking (10-12 min.). Shake them halfway through the cycle (5 min.).
5. Serve with a drizzle of lime juice as desired.

Cabbage Favorite

Servings: 4
Required Time: 15 minutes

Essential Ingredients:

- Cabbage (1 head)
- Olive oil (2 tbsp.)
- Coarse sea salt & black pepper (1 tsp. each)

Prep Method:

1. Warm the Air Fryer to 375° Fahrenheit/191° Celsius.
2. Slice the cabbage into two-inch slices – then quarter the slices.
3. Add them to the Air Fryer unit.
4. Spritz the cabbage using a spritz of oil and a dusting of pepper and salt.
5. Air-fry for five minutes
6. Toss the cabbage with tongs – pieces will fall apart into large chunks.
7. Continue to air-fry for three to four minutes to serve.

Delicious Corn-on-the-Cob

Servings: 4
Required Time: 12-15 minutes

Essential Ingredients:

- Corn (4 ears)
- Cooking spray or oil
- Salt and pepper (to your liking)

Prep Method:

1. Warm the fryer unit to 400° Fahrenheit/204° Celsius.
2. Husk and trim the corn. Spray or rub oil all over the prepared ears of corn. Place corn in the air fryer. If the ears of corn do not fit in your air fryer, breaking the ears of corn in half might help.
3. Cook for 8-10 minutes, flipping ears halfway through cook time.
4. Serve with butter and salt, and pepper to serve.

Mixed Veggies

Servings: 6
Required Time: 20 minutes

Essential Ingredients:

- Broccoli florets (1 cup)
- Baby carrots (.5 cup)
- Cauliflower florets (1 cup)
- Yellow squash (.5 cup)
- Baby zucchini (.5 cup)
- Mushrooms (.5 cup)
- Onion (1 small)
- Garlic cloves (1 tbsp.)
- Balsamic vinegar (.25 cup)
- Olive oil (1 tbsp.)
- Black pepper and sea salt (1 tsp. each)
- Parmesan cheese (.25 cup)
- Red pepper flakes (1 tsp.)

Prep Method:

1. Warm the Air Fryer to 400° Fahrenheit/204° Celsius for three minutes.
2. Slice the zucchini, squash, onions, and mushrooms. Mince the garlic.
3. Toss the oil with vinegar, salt, garlic, pepper, and red pepper flakes.
4. Whisk and add the veggies - tossing to coat. Air-fry for six to eight minutes.

5. Add cheese and air-fry for one to two minutes to serve.

Polenta Fries

Servings: 3
Time Required: 30 minutes

Essential Ingredients:

- Prepared polenta (16 oz. pkg.)
- Salt & pepper (as desired)
- Olive oil cooking spray (as needed)

Prep Method:

1. Preheat the fryer to 350° Fahrenheit/177° Celsius.
2. Prepare the polenta into thin slices and spritz the air fryer basket.
3. When ready, lightly spray about half the fries and dust with pepper and salt to cook (10 min.)
4. Flip and proceed to cook till you have reached the desired crispiness (5 min.). Scatter them over a few paper towels to absorb any excess fat.
5. Lastly, proceed with the second batch of fries.

Sweet Potato Fries

Servings: 4
Required Time: 30 minutes

Essential Ingredients:

- Olive oil (1 tbsp.)
- Black pepper and sea salt (.25 tsp. of each)
- Cinnamon (.25 tsp. each)
- Cayenne pepper (.25 tsp. each)
- Sweet potatoes (2 medium - peeled & sliced into 1/4-inch sticks)

Prep Method:

1. Set the fryer at 400° Fahrenheit/204° Celsius. Line a platter using several paper towels.
2. Lightly spray the Air Fryer basket using a spritz of cooking oil spray.
3. Whisk the oil with the salt, pepper, cayenne, and cinnamon in a big mixing container. Add sweet potatoes - toss thoroughly to coat.
4. Arrange the potatoes (single layer) in the prepared basket.
5. Air fry till they're browned and crispy (14 min.), flipping halfway through.
6. Scoop the fries onto the platter to drain.
7. Serve immediately.
8. Its diabetic exchange is one starch and ½ fat.

Veggie Frittata with Cheese

Servings: 4
Time Required: 23-25 minutes

Essential Ingredients:

- Mushrooms (1 cup)
- Leek (.25 cup)
- Spinach (1 cup)
- Eggs (4)
- Heavy cream (3 tbsp.)
- Shredded cheddar cheese (.5 cups)
- Regular & table salt (1 tsp. of each – as desired)
- Black pepper (.5 tsp.)
- As Required: Cooking oil spray

Prep Method:

1. Set the fryer at 300° Fahrenheit/149° Celsius.
2. Lightly spritz the pan with cooking spray.
3. Begin by dicing the leek, spinach, and mushrooms.
4. Whisk the egg, then add the veggies, other fixings, and cheese.
5. Add the mixture to the prepared pan to cook (10 min.) to serve.

Part 3: Meal Favorites - Other Methods

Many of these dishes would make a perfect luncheon favorite or side dish. You will be preparing this group of delicious recipes using various techniques which are fully explained. Also, consider low-fat types like ricotta, mozzarella, or cottage cheese which are high-protein choices that help keep your blood sugar manageable. You will see some of these also represented.

Chapter 8: Noodles & Other Specialties

Baked Zucchini Noodles with Cheese

Servings: 3
Time Required: 25 minutes

Essential Ingredients:

- Spiralized zucchini (2)
- Quartered plum tomato (1)
- Feta/your favorite cheese (8 cubes)
- Pepper and salt (1 tsp. of each)

- Olive oil (1 tbsp.)
- Cooking spray/oil (as needed)

Prep Method:

1. Lightly spritz a roasting pan with a small portion of cooking spray.
2. Set the oven temperature to 375° Fahrenheit/191° Celsius.
3. Slice the noodles with a spiralizer, and add the olive oil, tomatoes, pepper, and salt.
4. Bake the noodles in an oven-safe dish till they are fully cooked (10-15 min.).
5. Transfer from the oven and add the cheese cubes, tossing to combine. Serve.

Cabbage Patties

Servings: 4 or 8 patties
Time Required: 25 minutes

Essential Ingredients:

- Cabbage (3 cups)
- Egg (1 large)
- Coconut flour (.75 tbsp.)
- Coconut oil, melted (2 tbsp.)
- Optional: Garlic powder & salt

Prep Method:

1. Cook and finely chop the cabbage. Toss it with the seasonings and flour into a food processor. Pulse three to four times or until the coconut flour is evenly dispersed.
2. Crack the egg into the mixture and add the oil. Blend to combine thoroughly (3-4 pulses). Don't the cabbage too fine.
3. Roll the mixture into eight balls and flatten.
4. Lightly spray a skillet with a spritz of cooking oil spray or add additional fat. Add the patties and cook till they are done.
5. Serve the patties plain or top them off as desired.

Caprese Skewers

Servings: 2
Time Required: 5 minutes

Essential Ingredients:

- Baby mozzarella cheese balls (2 cups)
- Cherry or baby heirloom tomatoes (2 cups)
- Pitted mixed olives (.5 cup)
- Green/red pesto (2 tbsp.)
- Fresh basil (2 tbsp.)

Prep Method:

1. Rinse the basil and tomatoes.
2. Marinate the kalamata and green olives in extra-virgin olive oil with the oregano.
3. Combine the mozzarella with the pesto.
4. Arrange the olives, mozzarella, and tomatoes onto the skewers and garnish with basil.
5. Serve any time.

Cauliflower Fried Rice

Servings: 4
Time Required: 12-15 minutes

Essential Ingredients:

- Toasted sesame oil (1 tsp.)
- Riced cauliflower, fresh or frozen (12 oz.)
- Olive oil (2 tbsp.)
- Green onion (.25 cup)
- Carrot (.25 cup)
- Soy sauce (2 tbsp.)
- Egg (1 large)
- Garlic cloves (2)

Prep Method:

1. First, finely chop the carrot and onion as desired. Crush the garlic cloves.
2. Cook the carrots and the riced cauliflower in the olive oil over medium heat while occasionally stirring (5 min.).
3. Mix and stir in the garlic and the chopped green onion to sauté (1 min.).
4. Whisk and add the egg to the rice mix and stir just until the egg is scrambled throughout the rice (2-3 min.).
5. Just before serving, stir in the soy sauce and the sesame oil.

Cauliflower Hash Browns

Servings: 4
Time Required: 20 minutes

Essential Ingredients:

- Eggs (3 well-beaten)
- Yellow onion (1/2 of 1)
- Cauliflower (1 full head)
- Butter (4 tbsp.)
- Salt and pepper (1 tsp. each)

Prep Method:

1. Thoroughly rinse the cauliflower, let it drain thoroughly in a colander, and then pat dry.
2. Finely mince/grate the raw cauliflower using a hand grater or a food processor.
3. Place the cauliflower and onions into a bowl and add the egg, salt, and pepper. Thoroughly mix the fixings.
4. Use your hands to form the grated cauliflower mixture into pancake shapes and fry them in the melted butter for five minutes on each side.
5. Note: If they do not fry long enough, they will break apart when you flip them or remove them from the pan, so do not try to rush the process.

'Cauliflower Mac' & Cheese

Servings: 4
Time Required: 25-30 minutes

Essential Ingredients:

- Almond milk – unsweetened (.25 cup)
- Butter (3 tbsp.)
- Heavy cream (.25 cup)
- Cheddar/your favorite cheese (1 cup)
- Cauliflower (1 head)
- Sea salt & pepper (as desired)
- Also Needed: Parchment baking paper or foil

Prep Method:

1. First, prepare the cauliflower into small bite-sized florets. Then shred the cheese.
2. Preheat the oven to 450° Fahrenheit or 232° Celsius.
3. Cover a baking tray and set to the side for now.
4. Add butter (2 tbsp.) to a frying pan to melt, then add the cauliflower with a dusting of pepper and salt.
5. Lastly, arrange the cauliflower over the tray to roast (10-15 min.).
6. Retrieve a double boiler or use the microwave. Heat the remainder of the butter with the cheese, heavy cream, and milk.

7. Pour the sauce over the cauliflower to serve.

Edamame Kelp Noodles

Servings: 2
Time Required: 30 minutes

Essential Ingredients

- Kelp noodles (12 oz. pkg./as desired)
- Edamame – shelled (.5 cup)
- Carrots (.25 cup)
- Mushrooms (.25 cup)
- Frozen spinach (1 cup)

The Sauce:
- Sesame oil (1 tbsp.)
- Tamari (2 tbsp.)
- Ground ginger (.5 tsp.)
- Garlic powder (.5 tsp.)
- Sriracha (.25 tsp.)

Prep Method:

1. Do the prep. Soak the noodles in water and thoroughly drain. Julienne the carrots and slice the mushrooms.
2. Use a medium-temperature setting and place the sauce fixings in a saucepan. Add the veggies and warm.
3. Stir in the noodles and simmer while stirring occasionally (2-3 min.).

<u>Luncheon Cauliflower & Spinach Bowl</u>

Servings: 1
Time Required: 25-30 minutes

Essential Ingredients:

- Garlic (.25 tbsp.)
- Cauliflower (.75 cups)
- Almonds (.25 cup)
- Cilantro (.5 cup)
- Sunflower seeds (.5 tbsp.)
- Olive oil (2 tbsp.)
- Ricotta cheese (.5 tbsp.)

Prep Method:

1. Chop the garlic and cauliflower.
2. Preheat the oven at 375° Fahrenheit or 191° Celsius.
3. Add the almonds to a baking tray to roast (7-10 min.). Wait for a few minutes for them to cool.
4. Add the cauliflower to a food processor – working till it is rice-like.
5. In a medium heated skillet, warm some oil (1 tbsp.).
6. Add the 'riced' cauliflower and garlic. Sauté until golden brown, dusting with pepper and salt.
7. Toss in the cilantro and spinach, but don't stir -let them wilt on top (2-3 min.)

8. Garnish with sunflower seeds, almonds, and ricotta before serving.

Philly Cheesesteak Stuffed Peppers

Servings: 4
Time Required: 30 minutes

Essential Ingredients:

- Green peppers (4)
- Butter (1 tbsp.)
- Onions (.25 cup)
- Garlic (1 tsp.)
- Green peppers (.25 cup)
- Shaved beef steak (1 lb.)
- Salt & pepper (to taste) or Montreal steak seasoning
- Mayo – low-carb (2 tbsp.)
- Pepper jack/another cheese (7 slices)

Prep Method:

1. Remove and chop the tops from the peppers and place them into a 400° Fahrenheit or 204° Celsius oven.
2. Mince the garlic, chop the onions, and toss into a skillet with the butter, garlic, and (tops) chopped peppers. Sauté until softened.
3. Toss in the steak and seasonings of choice; chopping them apart as they cook. Add a slice of cheese and turn off the heat.

4. Transfer the peppers from the oven when softened just a little and stuff.
5. Add the mayonnaise to the steak and mix. Scoop into the pepper shells adding a piece of cheese to the top of all the stuffed peppers.
6. Broil until the cheese melts (5 min.). Serve with a smile.

Red Pepper Zoodles

Servings: 4
Time Required: 25 minutes

Essential Ingredients:

- Garlic (1 clove)
- Bell peppers - red (1)
- Almond milk (1 cup)
- Olive oil (1 tbsp.)
- Almond butter (.25 cup)
- Salt (1 tsp.)

Prep Method:

1. Prepare a baking sheet by lining it with foil.
2. Add the bell peppers to the baking sheet before placing them on the top level of your broiler and letting them cook until blackened. Remove and cool.
3. Once they have cooled, you can remove the skins, stems, seeds, and ribs.
4. Mix in the prepared mixture, and remaining sauce ingredients, and blend thoroughly. Season as desired. -
5. Serve with zoodles as well as a variety of potential toppings, including things like truffle oil, goat cheese, or parsley.

Vegetarian Sautéed Zucchini with Tomatoes

Servings: 5
Time Required: 20 minutes

Essential Ingredients:

- Zucchini (1 medium)
- Fresh plum tomatoes (5 medium)
- Garlic (5 cloves)
- Olive oil (2 tbsp.)
- Kosher salt & pepper (as desired)
- 'Herbes' de Provence (.5 tsp.)

Prep Method:

1. Use a big skillet to warm the oil using a med-high heat setting.
2. Dice the zucchini and tomatoes; set aside.
3. Mince and add the garlic and sauté until golden (1-2 min.).
4. Mix in the zucchini with a shake of pepper and salt.
5. Let the veggies simmer (4-6 min each side). Mix in the tomatoes, Herbes de Provence, and more salt as desired.
6. Adjust the temperature setting and simmer (5-10 min.).

Chapter 9: Other Favorite Meals

Do you question the safety of cheese? According to the pros, for diabetics, cheese is safe in moderation. When cheese is a part of a balanced, healthy diet, people with diabetes can do so without risk. A diet that contains too much cheese would be unhealthy for people of all ages, regardless of whether they have diabetes. As with other foods, moderation is crucial.

Soup Options

Burger Stew

Servings: 6
Required Time: 25-30 minutes

Essential Ingredients:

- Ground beef – lean suggested (1 lb. or 16 oz./453.5 g)
- Italian-style vegetables - frozen used (2 cups)
- Diced tomatoes with basil & garlic (14 oz. or 396.8 g can)
- Beef broth (14 oz. can.)
- Uncooked medium egg noodles (2.5 cups)
- Pepper & salt (as desired)

Prep Method:

1. Over medium-high heat, warm a frying pan.
2. Add the beef to brown, stirring as you break it apart (6-8 min). Then drain the fat.
3. Mix in the tomatoes, broth, and veggies using the high-temperature setting. Wait for it to boil.
4. Toss in the noodles and change the heat setting to medium.
5. Put a lid on the pot to simmer till the vegetables and noodles are tender (12-15 min.).
6. Now chop and sprinkle with parsley and a dusting of pepper and salt before serving.

Cauliflower Beef Curry

Servings: 4
Time Required: 30 minutes

Essential Ingredients:

- Cauliflower florets (1 head)
- Lean ground beef (1.5 lb./680 g)
- Olive oil (2 tbsp.)
- Allspice (.25 tsp.)
- Cumin (.5 tsp.)
- Garlic-ginger paste (1 tbsp.)
- Whole tomatoes (6 oz./170 g can)
- Chili pepper & salt (to your liking)
- Water (.25 cup)

Prep Method:

1. Heat the oil in a frying pan (medium temperature).
2. Add the meat to the skillet to fry (5 min.).
3. Mix in the cauliflower, tomatoes, allspice, salt, chili pepper, and cumin. Sauté it for six minutes.
4. Pour in the water and boil for ten minutes.
5. Serve it warm after the liquids have reduced by about half.

Colby Cauliflower Soup & Pancetta Chips

Servings: 4
Time Required: 20 minutes

Essential Ingredients:

- Cauliflower florets (2 heads)
- Onion (1)
- Ghee (2 tbsp.)
- Water (2 cups)
- Almond milk (3 cups)
- Shredded Colby cheese/or a preferred cheese (1 cup)
- Pancetta strips (3)

Prep Method:

1. Chop the cauliflower and onion. Shred the cheese.
2. Select a saucepan to fully melt the ghee (or butter if you choose).
3. Toss in the onion to sauté (3 min.). Mix in the cauliflower and sauté for three more minutes.
4. Pour in the water, salt, and pepper. Boil and lower the heat setting to simmer (10 min.).
5. Puree the cauliflower and mix in the cheese and milk. Once it's melted, adjust the seasonings to your liking.

6. Prepare the pancetta until crispy in a skillet. Toss it over the soup and serve.

Creamy Chicken Soup

Servings: 4
Time Required: 10-15 minutes

Essential Ingredients:

- Butter (2 tbsp.)
- Heavy cream (.25 cup)
- Large chicken breast (1-2 cups)
- Cream cheese – cubed – or a preferred cheese (4 oz./110 g)
- Garlic seasoning (2 tbsp.)
- Chicken broth (14.5 oz./410 g)
- Salt (as desired)

Prep Method:

1. Warm a saucepan using medium heat to melt the butter.
2. Shred and add in the chicken and toss with the cream cheese and seasoning.
3. When it is all melted, stir in the heavy cream and broth.
4. Once boiling, tweak the heat to simmer (3-4 min.).
5. Season the soup as desired before serving.

Creamy Pumpkin & Sausage Chowder

Servings: 8
Required Time: 30 minutes

Essential Ingredients:

- Chicken broth (4 cups)
- Solid pack pumpkin puree (1.25 cups)
- Pork sausage roll (1 lb./450 g)
- Water (3 cups)
- Dry sherry (.25 cup)
- Ground nutmeg (.25 tsp.)
- Kosher salt (1 tsp.)
- Black pepper (.25 tsp.)
- Onion and garlic powder (1 tsp. each)
- Cauliflower rice (3 cups)
- Freshly minced sage (1 tbsp.)

Prep Method:

1. Brown the sausage in a large saucepan while continuously stirring to make small chunks.
2. Pour in the chicken broth, water, pumpkin puree, sherry, nutmeg, pepper, garlic, salt, onion, and cauliflower. Simmer for 20 minutes.
3. Add the mascarpone cheese and sage.
4. Simmer the mixture (medium-low heat), stirring occasionally until the cheese has melted into the broth and is creamy smooth (5 min.). *Don't boil.*

5. Serve it while it is piping hot. Stored properly, enjoy it for about five days.

Curried-Style Fish Stew

Servings: 6
Time Required: 30 minutes

Essential Ingredients:

- Chopped onion (1 medium)
- Cauliflower (1 head - chopped)
- Olive oil (1 tbsp.)
- Garlic cloves (3)
- Curry powder (2 tbsp.)
- Fish/vegetable broth (2 cups)
- Firm - cubed whitefish – ex. halibut/cod (1.5 lb./680 g)
- Ground cayenne pepper (1 tsp.)
- Salt & pepper (as desired)
- Tomato paste (1 tbsp.)
- Coconut milk – full-fat used (13.5 oz./380 g can)

Prep Method:

1. First, warm the oil in a big saucepan using a medium temperature setting.
2. Mince and sauté the garlic and onion (5-7 min.).
3. Once they're translucent, stir in the curry powder, cauliflower, and tomato paste. Continue sauteing, adding the cayenne, pepper, and salt (10-15 min. as needed).

4. Pour in the coconut milk and simmer using the low setting till it is ready to serve.
5. Store in the refrigerator for up to four days.

Egg Drop Soup

Servings: 6
Time Required: 20-25 minutes

Essential Ingredients:

- Vegetable broth (2 quarts)
- Fresh ginger (1 tbsp.)
- Turmeric (1 tbsp.)
- Chili pepper (1 small)
- Coconut aminos (2 tbsp.)
- Garlic cloves (2)
- Eggs (4 large)
- Mushrooms (2 cups/150 g)
- Chopped spinach (4 cups/900 g)
- Spring onions (2 medium)
- Fresh cilantro (2 tbsp.)
- Black pepper (as desired)
- Pink Himalayan salt (1 tsp.)
- To Serve: Olive oil (6 tbsp.)

Prep Method:

1. Prepare the fixings. Grate the ginger root and turmeric. Mince the cloves of garlic. Then slice the mushrooms and peppers.
2. Chop the chard stalks and leaves. Separate the stalks from the leaves. Dump the vegetable stock into a soup pot and simmer until it begins to boil.
3. Toss in the garlic, ginger, turmeric, chard stalks, mushrooms, coconut

aminos, and chili peppers. Boil for approximately five minutes.
4. Fold in the chard leaves and simmer for one minute.
5. Whip the eggs in a dish and add them slowly to the soup mixture. Stir until the egg is done and set it on the counter.
6. Slice the onions and chop the cilantro. Toss them into the pot.
7. Pour into serving bowls and drizzle with some olive oil (1 tbsp. per serving).

Green Chicken Enchilada Soup

Servings: 4
Time Required: 9-11 minutes

Essential Ingredients:

- Room temperature cream cheese (4 oz. or 110 g)
- Cooked chicken - shredded (2 cups)
- Salsa Verde (.5 cup)
- Sharp cheddar cheese/your favorite - shredded (1 cup)
- Chicken stock (2 cups)

Prep Method:

1. Load the blender with the cream and cheddar cheese, salsa, and chicken stock. Mix until smooth. Alternatively, you can use an immersion blender in the saucepan.
2. Pour the soup into a saucepan and cook using the medium-temperature setting until hot – don't bring it to a boil. On the other hand, you can heat it in a microwave-safe bowl for one-minute increments until hot, stirring fully in between each minute.
3. Mix in the shredded chicken - continue cooking (3-5 min.) until heated.
4. Garnish with additional shredded cheddar and chopped cilantro as desired.

Green Soup

Servings: 6
Time Required: 6-8 minutes

Essential Ingredients:

- Spinach leaves (2 cups)
- Diced avocado (1)
- Diced English cucumber (.5 cup)
- Gluten-free vegetable broth (.25 cup)
- Black pepper and salt (as desired)

Prep Method:

1. Combine each of the fixings in the blender.
2. Toss in the fresh herbs and serve.

Mushroom-Kale & Sausage Soup

Servings: 6
Time Required: 5 minutes (+) simmer time

Essential Ingredients:

- Fresh kale (6.5 oz. or 180 g)
- Mushrooms (6.5 oz.)
- Chicken bone broth (29 oz. or 820 g)
- Sausage (1 lb. or 450 g)
- Garlic (2 cloves)

Prep Method:

1. Chop the kale into edible chunks. Then slice the mushrooms and mince the garlic.
2. Now, discard the casings and cook the sausage.
3. Pour in the broth with two cans of water.
4. Set the burner to medium and boil the mixture.
5. Toss in the rest of the fixings and simmer for one hour using the low-temperature setting.

Pumpkin Soup

Servings: 5
Time Required: 20-25 minutes

Essential Ingredients:

- Coconut milk (1 cup)
- Chicken bone broth (2 cups)
- Baked pumpkin or canned pumpkin (6 cups/2 - 13 oz./370 g cans)
- Pepper and sea salt (as desired)

Chosen Spices @ 1 tsp. each:
- Ground cinnamon
- Garlic powder
- Paprika
- Dried ginger
- Nutmeg

Optional Toppings:
- Sour cream
- Toasted pumpkin seeds

Prep Method:

1. Heat a soup pot using medium heat and add the milk, broth, pumpkin, and spices. Simmer while stirring (15 min.).
2. Use an immersion blender to mix if using fresh pumpkin until creamy (1 min.).

3. Note: If the soup is too thin, simmer it on a med-low temperature setting, uncovered, until it thickens to desired consistency.
4. Garnish using coconut yogurt or sour cream. Top using a few pumpkin seeds and serve.

Shirataki Soup

Servings: 2
Time Required: 20-25 minutes

Essential Ingredients:

- Boneless - skinless chicken thighs (2)
- Chicken stock (3 cups)
- Minced ginger (1 tsp.)
- Cardamom (.25 tsp.)
- Minced garlic (1 clove)
- Mushrooms (.5 cup)
- Optional: Chili sauce (1 tsp.)
- Chopped cilantro (1 pinch)
- Thinly sliced chili pepper (1)

Prep Method:

1. Heat the stock (medium-high) on the stovetop. Toss in the ginger, garlic, mushrooms, and cardamom. Simmer for about ten minutes.
2. Fold in the chicken and cook until done or about five minutes.
3. Prepare two soup bowls and add the sliced chili pepper to each dish. Serve the soup and garnish with some cilantro.
4. Adjust spices as desired.

Spicy Cauliflower Soup

Servings: 6
Required Time: 20 minutes

Essential Ingredients:

- Cauliflower (1 large @ 800 g or 1.7 lb.)
- Turnip* (200 g or 7.1 oz)
- White onion - chopped (70 g or 1 small)
- Chicken/ vegetable stock/bone broth (2 cups or 480 ml/ 16 fl. oz.)
- Pepperoni or Medium Spanish chorizo sausage (1 @ 150 g or 5.3 oz)
- Butter/ghee (3 tbsp. or 45 g or 1.6 oz)
- Sea salt (.5 tsp.)
- To Garnish: Medium spring onion or chives (15 g or as desired)

Prep Method:

1. Thoroughly rinse the cauliflower and slice into small chunks.
2. *Note: Use more cauliflower if you do not like turnip.
3. Lightly grease a large soup pot with ghee (2 tbsp.). Finely mince and toss in the onion to sauté - med-high temperature setting - till it is slightly browned.
4. Toss in the cauliflower and sauté while stirring (5 min.).
5. Mix in the stock, put a top on the pot, and simmer (10 min.).
6. Meanwhile, mince or chop the sausage.

7. Remove the turnip peel and finely chop the turnip/cauliflower – stems also.
8. Use a cast-iron skillet (if available) lightly greased with the rest of the ghee.
9. Sauté it using a med-high temperature setting till the turnip is tender and the meat is crispy (8-10 min.).
10. Scoop about half of the chorizo/turnip mixture with cayenne and salt into the soup.
11. Now, prepare it with a hand blender till it is velvety. Or you can either add one cup of heavy whipping cream or grated cheddar cheese.
12. Serve the soup with more of the chorizo and turnip mixture. Lastly spritz it with the spicy oil topped as desired.

Salad Favorites

Avocado & Tomato Salad Specialty

Servings: 4
Required Time: 15 minutes

Essential Ingredients:

- Dijon mustard (1 tsp.)
- Olive oil (.25 cup)
- Vinegar – balsamic used (.5 cup)
- Pepper (1 pinch)
- Small tomatoes (2)
- Avocado (1)

Prep Method:

1. Whisk the mustard with pepper, oil, and vinegar.
2. Peel, remove the pit and slice the avocado. Slice each of the tomatoes into eight wedges.
3. Alternate the wedges of veggies on a serving dish.
4. Lightly spritz it using the dressing and serve promptly.

Balsamic Blackberry & Spinach Salad

Servings: 6
Time Required: 15 minutes

Essential Ingredients:

- Baby spinach (3 cups)
- Fresh blackberries (2 cups)
- Cherry tomatoes (1.5 cups)
- Crumbled feta cheese (.33 or 1/3 cup)
- Green onions (2)
- Toasted walnuts (.25 cup)
- Balsamic vinaigrette (.33 cup)

Prep Method:

1. First, halve the berries and tomatoes. Thinly slice the onions and chop the nuts.
2. Toss the salad fixings into a mixing container.
3. Portion into six serving dishes and serve with a splash of dressing as desired.

Brussel Sprout Salad

Servings: 2
Time Required: 10 minutes

Essential Ingredients:

- Brussels sprouts (6)
- Grapeseed or olive oil (1 tsp.)
- Vinegar – apple-cider used (.5 tsp.)
- Salt & black pepper (to taste)
- Shredded parmesan (1 tbsp.)

Prep Method:

1. Thoroughly rinse the brussels sprouts.
2. Slice the sprouts in half, the long way, cutting through the root. However, do not slice entirely to remove its roots since that is what holds the leaves in place.
3. Thinly slice it in the opposite direction across. Now, discard the root.
4. Add the sprouts to a dish and break them into pieces. Add the oil, apple cider, pepper, and salt. Lastly, dust with the parmesan cheese and toss to serve.

Caprese Salad

Servings: 2
Time Required: 5 minutes

Essential Ingredients:

- Fresh mozzarella (.5 lb. or 230 g)
- Tomato (1 large)
- Balsamic reduction (1 tbsp.)
- Olive oil (1 tbsp.)
- Basil (4 leaves)
- Pepper and salt (1 pinch each)

Prep Method:

1. Slice/dice the cheese and the tomatoes. Intertwine them in the serving dish.
2. Sprinkle as desired with the balsamic reduction and oil.
3. Garnish as desired.

Chicken & Apple Creamy-Style Salad

Servings: 8
Time Required: 15 minutes

Essential Ingredients:

- Cooked breast of chicken (2 cups)
- Celery (2 stalks)
- Green onions (2)
- Medium apple (1)
- Walnuts (3 tbsp.)
- Light mayo (.25 cup)
- Yogurt– fat-free – plain (.25 cup)
- Lemon (half of 1)
- Black pepper (.125 or 1/8 tsp.)

Prep Method:

1. Chop the chicken, celery, apple, and onions. Juice the lemon. Chop the nuts.
2. Toss the nuts with the apple, onions, celery, and chicken.
3. In another container, whisk the mayo with the pepper, juiced lemon, mayo, and yogurt.
4. Dump the mixture over the chicken while gently stirring to cover.
5. Serve with a few crackers, bread, or over lettuce leaves.

Chicken & Berry Salad

Servings: 2
Time Required: 10-15 minutes

Essential Ingredients:

- Chicken breast (1)
- Chopped walnuts (.5 cup)
- Diced strawberries (6)
- Spinach (2 cups)
- Blueberries (.75 cup)
- Raspberry balsamic vinegar (3 tbsp.)
- Crumbled feta cheese (3 tbsp.)

Prep Method:

1. Slice the chicken into cubes and cook in a skillet.
2. Dice, chop, crumble, and mix in the remainder of the fixings in a salad container.
3. Combine with the chicken and dressing. Toss and enjoy.

Chicken-Pecan Salad & Cucumber Bites

Servings: 2
Time Required: 8-10 minutes

Essential Ingredients:

- Cucumber (1)
- Precooked chicken breast (1 cup)
- Celery (.25 cup)
- Mayo – diabetic-friendly (2 tbsp.)
- Pecans (.25 cup)

Prep Method:

1. Discard the peeling - then slice the cucumber into 1/4-inch slices. Dice the chicken and celery. Chop the pecans.
2. Mix the pecans, chicken, mayonnaise, and celery in a salad bowl. Dust the mixture using a bit of salt and pepper to your liking.
3. Prepare the cucumber slices. Layer each one with a spoonful of the chicken salad to serve.

Chopped Greek Salad

Servings: 2
Required Time: 5 minutes

Essential Ingredients:

- Olive oil (1 tbsp.)
- Chopped romaine (2 cups)
- Kalamata black olives (.25 cup)
- Halved grape tomatoes (.5 cup)
- Crumbled feta cheese (.25 cup)
- Vinaigrette dressing (2 tbsp.)
- Pepper and pink salt (as desired)

Prep Method:

1. Prepare the salad with the romaine as a base. Drizzle it with oil and vinegar.
2. Serve it in two salad dishes.

Cucumber Avocado Salad

Servings: 4
Time Required: 25 minutes

Essential Ingredients:

- Shallot (1 medium - sliced crosswise & separated into rings)
- Fresh lime juice (3 tbsp.)
- Salt (.5 tsp.)
- English cucumber (1)
- Ripe avocado - halved - pitted & sliced crosswise (1)
- Fresh basil & mint (1 tbsp. each)
- Olive oil (3 tbsp.)

+

Prep Method:

1. Thinly slice the cucumber, shallot, basil, and mint. Make the rings by slicing them crosswise.
2. Toss the shallot rings with lime juice in a large bowl, waiting till they are softened (10 min.).
3. Now, whisk in oil, basil, mint, and salt. Lastly, add the cucumber while tossing it gently to cover. Toss occasionally till it is softened (10 min.).
4. Scoop the deliciously prepared cucumber onto a platter, topped with

the avocado and a drizzle of dressing to serve.

Curry Egg Salad

Servings: 4
Time Required: 15 minutes

Essential Ingredients:

- Hard-boiled eggs (6)
- Curry powder (1 tsp. or to taste)
- Mayo – diabetic-friendly (.5 cup)

Prep Method:

1. Prepare the boiled eggs by adding them to a saucepan. Pour in cold water. Turn the burner on.
2. Wait for the water to boil and set a timer for seven minutes.
3. Empty the hot water and place the eggs in a cold water/ice dish to hinder the cooking process.
4. Once they're cool, peel and chop the eggs into small bits.

Greek Lamb Meatball Salad

Servings: 4
Time Required: 20 minutes

Essential Ingredients:

- Finely chopped mint (.25 cup)
- Garlic cloves (2 minced)
- Pepper and salt (to your liking)
- Dried oregano (2 tsp.)
- Ground lamb (1 lb./450 g)
- Olive oil (4 tbsp.)

The Salad:
- Lettuce leaves (2-3)
- Tomato (1)
- Lemon (1)
- Chopped flat-leaf parsley (.25 cup)

Prep Method:

1. Warm the oven to 350° Fahrenheit/177° Celsius.
2. Slice the tomato and lemon into wedges.
3. Combine the spices and meat and shape them into meatballs. Portion the mixture for four servings.
4. Heat the oil in a frying pan till the meatballs are lightly browned. Arrange on a baking tin. Cook them for ten minutes.

5. Serve over the prepared salad with a garnish of lemon and parsley.

Green Bean Balsamic Salad

Servings: 16
Time Required: 30 minutes (+) chilling time

Essential Ingredients:

- Fresh green beans (2 lb.)
- Olive oil (.25 cup)
- Lemon juice (3 tbsp.)
- Pepper (.125 or ⅛ tsp.)
- Salt (.25 tsp.)
- Garlic powder & salt (.25 tsp. of each)
- Ground mustard (.25 tsp.)
- Balsamic vinegar (3 tbsp.)
- Red onion (1 large)
- Cherry tomatoes (4 cups - halved)
- Crumbled feta cheese (1 cup/4 oz.)
- Suggested: 6-quart stockpot

Prep Method:

1. Trim the beans into 1.5-inch pieces. Then, toss them into the pot and cover with water.
2. Cover and simmer till tender and crispy (8-10 min.). Immediately drain into a pan of ice water, drain, and pat dry (after they are chilled).
3. Whisk the oil with mustard, pepper, garlic powder, salt, vinegar, and lemon juice. Drizzle over the drained beans.

4. Chop and add in the onion, tossing to cover.
5. Place them in the refrigerator for about one hour.
6. At serving time, mix in the tomatoes and cheese.

Green Salad with Beets & Edamame

Servings: 1
Time Required: 14-15 minutes

Essential Ingredients:

- Mixed salad greens (2 cups)
- Thawed & shelled edamame (1 cup)
- Raw beet - peeled & shredded (about 1/2 cup or half of 1 medium)
- Red-wine vinegar (1 tbsp. + 1.5 tsp.)
- Freshly chopped cilantro (1 tbsp.)
- Olive oil (2 tsp.)
- Black pepper (to your liking)

Prep Method:

1. Arrange the greens, edamame, and beet on a large plate.
2. Whisk vinegar with the pepper, salt, cilantro, and oil in a mixing container.
3. Drizzle over the salad and enjoy.

Jar Salad on the Go for Vegans

Servings: 1
Time Required: 6-8 minutes

Essential Ingredients:

- Black pepper & salt (as desired)
- Diabetic-friendly mayo (4 tbsp.)
- Scallion (1)
- Cucumber (.25 oz./7 g)
- Red bell pepper (.25 oz.)
- Cherry tomatoes (.25 oz.)
- Leafy greens (.25 oz.)
- Seasoned tempeh (4 oz./110 g)

Prep Method:

1. Chop or shred the vegetables as desired.
2. Layer in the dark leafy greens first, followed by the onions, tomato, bell peppers, avocado, and shredded carrot.
3. Top with the tempeh, or use the same amount of another high-protein option to mix things up in later weeks.
4. Top with diabetic-vegan-friendly mayonnaise before serving.

Lobster Salad

Servings: 4
Time Required: 10-15 minutes

Essential Ingredients:

- Melted butter (.25 cup)
- Cooked lobster meat (1 lb.)
- Mayonnaise – low-cal (.25 cup/57.5 g)
- Black pepper (.125 tsp.)

Prep Method:

1. Chop the lobster into small edible pieces.
2. Melt and pour the butter over the meat. Toss to cover.
3. Blend in the mayo along with the pepper.
4. Chill in a covered dish for a minimum of 10 minutes or chilled to your liking.

Mustard Sardines Salad

Servings: 1
Time Required: 4-5 minutes

Essential Ingredients:

- Sardines in olive oil - low-salt (4-5 oz. or 110-140 g can)
- Lemon juice (1 tbsp.)
- Cucumber (¼ of 1)
- Mustard (.5 tbsp.)
- Black pepper & salt (as desired)

Prep Method:

1. Drain the bulk of the oil from the sardines and mash them.
2. Mix in the diced cucumbers, juice, pepper, salt, and mustard.
3. Spread the mixture out over some lettuce leaves for a treat.

Niçoise Salad

Servings: 1
Time Required: 15-20 minutes (or less)

Essential Ingredients:

- Large egg (1)
- Celery (.5 cup/115 g)
- Snow peas (.5 cup/75 g)
- Olive oil (2 tbsp.)
- Garlic (.25 tbsp.)
- Romaine lettuce (1 cup/75 g)
- Green onion (.5 tbsp.)
- Olives (.5 tbsp.)
- Crumbled feta cheese (.5 cup/75 g)
- Balsamic vinegar (1 tbsp.)

Prep Method:

1. Hard boil the egg and remove the peel when cooled.
2. Chop the garlic, onion, celery, and olives.
3. Warm oil in a frying pan to sauté the garlic, olives, and snow peas until the peas are bright green.
4. Prepare a large salad bowl and add the cooked veggies, shredded lettuce, celery, and green onion.
5. Whisk the oil, vinegar, pepper, and salt for the dressing.

6. Combine the fixings and toss well before serving.

Rosemary Tomato Salad

Servings: 4
Required Time: 20 minutes

Essential Ingredients:

- Vinegar – red wine type used (2 tbsp.)
- Olive oil (.25 cup)
- Fresh rosemary (1 sprig)
- Dried oregano (.125 or ⅛ tsp.)
- Pepper and kosher salt (as desired)
- Heirloom tomatoes (3 large + 3 small)

Prep Method:

1. First, finely dice the rosemary.
2. Whisk the oil with vinegar, oregano, and rosemary in a big mixing container.
3. Quarter the large tomatoes and combine them with the smaller ones while tossing them till they are fully covered.
4. Pop them in the fridge to chill (10-15 min.).
5. Toss again before serving with pepper and salt to your liking.

Scallion & Snap Pea Salad

Servings: 1
Time Required: 10-15 minutes

Essential Ingredients:

- Sugar snap peas (1.8 oz./50 g)
- Scallions - green & white parts (10 g/0.4 oz.)
- Sesame oil (2 g/0.1 oz.)
- Coconut aminos/or another keto-friendly soy sauce (2 g/0.1 oz.)
- Cider vinegar (3 g/0.1 oz.)
- Olive oil (11 g/0.4 oz.)
- Garlic powder (0.1 g/as desired)
- Sesame seeds (2 g/0.1 oz)
- Optional Ingredient: Red chili flakes

Prep Method:

1. Slice the snap peas and diagonally slice the scallions.
2. Combine the sliced veggies with the rest of the fixings, tossing thoroughly to combine.
3. Use a layer of plastic wrap to cover the container. Put the container in the fridge for at least two hours.
4. Serve with a choice of protein, such as grilled chicken, shrimp, or salmon. Heat if desired.

Shrimp & Avocado Salad

Servings: 6
Time Required: 20 minutes

Essential Ingredients:

- Ripe avocados (2 medium)
- Cooked shrimp (1.5 lb./680 g @ 31-40 per lb.)
- Pico de Gallo (1 cup)
- Hot pepper sauce (.25 tsp./less if desired)
- Clamato juice (.5 cup - chilled)
- Lime juice (2 tbsp.)
- Kosher salt (.25 tsp.)
- Ground cumin (.25 tsp.)
- Black pepper (1 dash)
- Optional: Lime wedges

Prep Method:

1. Eliminate the peeling and slice the avocado (½-inch chunks).
2. Peel, devein the shrimp, and remove the tails.
3. Toss all the fixings into a large mixing container.
4. Portion the salad and serve.

Tuna Salad & Chives

Servings: 4
Time Required: 5 minutes

Essential Ingredients:

- Tuna - packed in olive oil (15 oz. or 430 g)
- Mayo – low-cal (6 tbsp.)
- Chives (2 tbsp.)
- Pepper (.25 tsp.)

Prep Method:

1. Drain the tuna and finely chop the chives.
2. Add all the fixings except the lettuce into a mixing bowl.
3. Toss well. Enjoy as-is or spoon into romaine lettuce leaves.

Dressing & Condiment Options

Alfredo Sauce

Servings: 6
Time Required: 10-13 minutes

Essential Ingredients:

- Unsalted butter (.5 cup)
- Garlic (2 cloves)
- Heavy whipping cream (2 cups)
- Room temperature cream cheese (half of a 4 oz. pkg)
- Grated parmesan cheese (1.5 cups)
  Spices as Desired (1 pinch of each):
- Salt
- Ground nutmeg
- Ground white pepper

Prep Method:

1. Preheat a saucepan to melt the butter. Chop and add the garlic and sauté it (2 min.).
2. Pour in the cream and cream cheese.
3. Slowly add the parmesan until the sauce is thickened (5-7 min.)
4. Stir it thoroughly and serve with white pepper, nutmeg, and salt.

Avocado Sauce

Time Required: 5 minutes

Essential Ingredients:

- Pistachio nuts (2 oz.)
- Avocado (1)
- Parsley or cilantro, fresh (1 cup)
- Lime juice (.25 cup)
- Salt (1 tsp.)
- Water (.25 cup)
- Olive oil (.66 or 2/3 cup)
- Garlic, minced (2 tbsp.)
- Suggested: Food processor or high-powered mixer

Prep Method:

1. First, mince the garlic.
2. Blend all the fixings till they are smooth. Omit the oil and the nuts. Add these at the end and mix everything together very well.
3. If the mix is a bit thick, you can add in a bit more oil or water.
4. This sauce will stay fresh in the refrigerator for up to four days.

BBQ Sauce

Servings: 16
Time Required: 17-20 minutes

Essential Ingredients:

- Sugar-free ketchup (.75 cup)
- Apple cider vinegar (1 tbsp.)
- Liquid smoke (1 tsp.)
- Yellow mustard (1 tbsp.)
- Smoked paprika (1.5 tsp.)
- Brown sugar substitute – ex. such as Swerve (2 tbsp.)
- Salt (.5 tsp.)
- Garlic powder (1 tsp.)

Prep Method:

1. Measure and add the mustard with the ketchup, brown sugar substitute, and vinegar in a saucepan. Let the mixture simmer for five minutes.
2. Lower the temperature setting to low and add paprika, liquid smoke, garlic powder, and salt.
3. Cook for an additional five minutes until thickened.

Brown Gravy with Zero Carbs

Servings: 8
Time Required: 10 minutes

Essential Ingredients:

- Unsalted butter/butter substitute for dairy-free (.25 cup)
- Organic Vegetable Broth - ex. Pacific Foods (2 cups) or Turkey drippings (1 cup)
- Garlic powder (1 tsp.)
- Black pepper (.25 tsp.)
- Sea salt (1 tsp.)
- Xanthan gum (1 tsp.)
- Also Needed: 10-inch cast-iron skillet

Prep Method:

1. Warm the skillet to melt the butter using the medium temperature setting.
2. Whisk the xanthan gum, salt, and garlic pepper to add it into the skillet.
3. Pour in the vegetable broth and simmer.
4. Serve when it's thickened, or save some for later.
5. Reheat it using the same process.

Caesar Dressing

Time Required: 5 minutes

Essential Ingredients:

- Lemon juice (1 tbsp.)
- Olive oil (.5 cup)
- Parmesan cheese - grated (.25 cup)
- Anchovies (1 oz.)
- Apple cider vinegar (1 tsp.)
- Dijon mustard (1 tbsp.)
- Salt (.5 tsp.)
- Garlic - minced (1 tsp.)
- Black pepper (.25 tsp.)

Prep Method:

1. First, mince the garlic. Then prepare and measure the remainder of the fixings.
2. To make the dressing, combine all the ingredients in a blender.
3. You can add a few drops of water to the dressing to thin it down if it appears a little too thick.
4. Enjoy the mixture for up to three days.

Classic Guacamole

Servings: 4
Time Required: 15 minutes

Essential Ingredients:

- Hass Avocado - mashed (230 g/1 cup)
- Cilantro (.25 cup/4 g)
- Spring onion (10 g/1 tbsp.)
- Jalapeño pepper (14 g/medium)
- Lime juice (15 g/1 tbsp.)
- Garlic (2.8 g/1 tsp.)
- Avocado oil (15 g/1 tbsp.)
- Salt (as desired)

Prep Method:

1. Thinly slice the spring onion. Mince the garlic, jalapeno, and cilantro.
2. Toss each of the fixings into a mixing container to thoroughly mix.
3. Add a layer of plastic cling wrap over the guacamole, pressing to remove air, and add a lid to the container.
4. Pop it into the fridge to chill.

Creamy Mushroom Sauce

Servings: 4
Time Required: 25-30 minutes

Essential Ingredients:

- Mushrooms (7 oz.)
- Fresh tarragon (2 tbsp.)
- Butter (1 tbsp.)
- Small onion (1)
- Garlic clove (1)
- Salt (.5 tsp.)
- Black pepper (1 pinch)
- Worcestershire sauce (5 tsp.)
- Dijon mustard (1 tbsp.)
- Heavy cream (.5 cup)

Prep Method:

1. Thinly slice the mushrooms, tarragon, and onions. Mince the garlic.
2. On the stovetop, prepare a saucepan using the high-heat temperature setting. Toss in the butter, onion, salt, pepper, and garlic. Sauté until the onions are translucent.
3. Mix in the mushrooms and sauté for three more minutes before lowering the temperature setting to low.
4. Combine the mustard, Worcestershire sauce, and cream. Simmer until the sauce thickens (10-15 minutes).

Enchilada Sauce

Time Required: 10-12 minutes

Essential Ingredients:

- Butter (3 oz. - salted)
- Cayenne (.25 tsp.)
- Dried oregano (2 tsp.)
- Cumin, ground (3 tsp.)
- Coriander, ground (2 tsp.)
- Onion powder (2 tsp.)
- <u>Erythritol</u> (1.5 tbsp.)
- Tomato puree - only tomatoes and salt (12 oz.)
- Salt and pepper (.5 tsp.)

Prep Method:

1. Prepare a saucepan to melt the butter using the medium temperature setting.
2. Add each of the fixings - excluding the tomato puree- and sauté them for about three minutes.
3. Add in the puree and simmer the sauce for about five minutes. Thin with water as needed.
4. Use it immediately or store it in a heatproof jar. It remains delicious for about two weeks.

Garlic-Parmesan Wing Sauce

Time Required: 5-6 minutes

Essential Ingredients:

- Unsalted butter (.25 cup)
- *Refrigerated fresh-type - grated parmesan (.5 cup)
- Onion & garlic powder (1 tsp. each)
- Dried parsley (1 tsp.)
- Black pepper (.25 tsp.)

Prep Method:

1. First, melt the butter.
2. *Note: If you are using unrefrigerated parmesan, be sure to use unsalted butter & cut the salt in half.
3. Mix all the ingredients for the sauce by stirring them in a small bowl. Salt is up to your preference.
4. Toss the wings in the garlic parmesan mixture and serve immediately.

Marinara Sauce

Servings: 2
Time Required: 8 minutes

Essential Ingredients:

- Olive oil (2 tbsp.)
- Clove of garlic – chopped and crushed (2 @ 1 of each)
- Oregano (2 tsp.)
- Tomato puree (16 oz.)
- Monk fruit (2 tsp.)
- Pepper and salt (1 tsp. of each)

Prep Method:

1. Add the olive oil and garlic into a medium or large saucepan.
2. Sauté using low to medium heat until fragrant (3 min.).
3. Add the tomato puree and stir well.
4. Mix in the oregano, monk fruit, pepper, and salt. Stir and chill the sauce.
5. Store in the fridge or eat immediately with your favorite low-carb pasta.

Mayonnaise

Servings: 1.25 cups @ 2 tbsp. each portion
Time Required: 5 minutes

Essential Ingredients:

- Salt (.5 tsp.)
- Dry mustard (1 tsp.)
- Avocado or olive oil (1.25 cups - divided)
- Egg – room-temperature (1)
- Fresh lemon juice – room-temp (2 tbsp.)

Prep Method:

1. Using a food processor, mix the mustard, salt, egg, juice, and 1/4 cup of the oil.
2. Process and slowly drizzle in the rest of the chosen oil. For the last two tablespoons - add quickly.

No-Cook Avocado Hollandaise

Servings: 4
Time Required: 5-6 minutes

Essential Ingredients:

- Ripe avocado (1 diced)
- Juice of 1 lemon
- Olive oil (.25 cup)
- Cayenne pepper (1 pinch)
- Kosher salt and freshly cracked black pepper

Prep Method:

1. In a blender or food processor, puree the avocado, lemon juice, and ⅓ cup water until combined.
2. With the motor running, add the olive oil in a slow stream and puree until the mixture has thickened with a creamy smooth texture.
3. Finish the hollandaise with cayenne, salt, and pepper. Serve it immediately.

Onion Gravy for Meat

Servings: 8 @ 2 tbsp. portions
Time Required: 20-25 minutes

Essential Ingredients:

- Water/pan drippings/meat stock (2 cups)
- Egg yolks (2 large)
- Onion (.5 cup)
- Butter or butter-flavored coconut oil (.25 cup)
- Pepper and salt (to your liking)
- Also Helpful: High-speed or stick blender

Prep Method:

1. Strain your pan drippings and add enough water or stock to make the two cups of liquid. Pour it into a saucepan and boil it to thicken (10 min.).
2. Add the onion and use the blender until it's pureed, and continue cooking.
3. Take it from the burner. Pour and whisk about ¼ cup of the liquid into the yolks of the egg.
4. Whisk it all together until smooth and simmer until it's the way you like it.
5. Note: The gravy will thicken as it cools if you use coconut oil, but the butter is better to thicken it. You can also add xanthan gum, coconut flour, or gelatin

to thicken the gravy if you want it thicker (a great cheat technique).

Pesto-Basil Sauce

Servings: 4
Time Required: 4-5 minutes

Essential Ingredients:

- Tamari (4 tbsp.)
- Natural - smooth peanut butter (2 tbsp.)
- Frank's Hot Sauce/your favorite (1 tsp.)
- Rice wine vinegar (2 tsp.)
- Clove of garlic (1)
- Pepper (1 pinch)
- Sesame oil (3 tsp.)
- Xanthan gum (.125 tsp.)
- Chinese five-spice (.25 tsp.)
- Sugar-free maple syrup (2 tsp.)

Prep Method:

1. Toss all the fixings into a blender.
2. Thoroughly mix until the sauce has thickened (2-3 min.)
3. It will keep in the refrigerator for up to three weeks.

Ranch Seasoning Mix

Time Required: 5 minutes

Essential Ingredients:

- Onion - minced - dry (2 tsp.)
- Dry powdered buttermilk (1/3 cup)

    Dry Spices:
- Parsley (2 tbsp.)
- Garlic powder (2 tsp.)
- Dill weed (1.5 tsp.)
- Chives (1 tsp.)
- Onion powder (2 tsp.)
- Pepper & salt (1 tsp. each)

Prep Method:

1. Toss the fixings and use the seasoning on pork chops and more.
2. It's easy to make a batch, then store it in the refrigerator until needed.

Tahini Dressing

Servings: 7 @ 1 tbsp. per portion
Time Required: 10 minutes

Essential Ingredients:

- Tahini (2 tbsp. or 30 g)
- Sweetener & salt (as desired)
- Olive oil (45 g or 3 tbsp.)
- Lemon juice (2 tbsp. or 30 g)
- Garlic powder (.5 tsp. or 2.5 g)

Prep Method:

1. Toss all the fixings in a small mixing container. Whisk until mixed.
2. Keep it fresh in a closed jar in the refrigerator.

White Wine Mustard

Servings: 12
Time Required: 10 minutes (+) 10 hours to chill

Essential Ingredients:

- Yellow mustard seeds - whole (3 tbsp.)
- Brown mustard seeds - whole (2.5 tbsp.)
- Dry white wine (.33 or ⅓ cup)
- White wine vinegar (.33 cup)
- Shallot/your preference (1)
- Ground allspice (1 pinch)
- Kosher salt (1 tsp.)
- White pepper - ground (.25 tsp.)

Prep Method:

1. First, mince the onion. Toss the fixings in a glass mixing bowl.
2. Cover it using a piece of plastic wrap and pop it in the fridge overnight for the best results.
3. When ready to use it, just dump it into a blender and pulse till it is as you desire to enjoy.

Vinaigrette Options

Asian Vinaigrette

Servings: 6
Time Required: 5 minutes

Essential Ingredients:

- Rice vinegar (.25 cup)
- Soy sauce or tamari – low-sodium suggested (1.5 tbsp.)
- Fresh ginger (.5 tbsp.)
- Garlic (half of 1 clove)
- Olive oil - extra-virgin preferred (.33 or 1/3 cup)
- Sriracha sauce (as desired)
- Black pepper

Prep Method:

1. First, mince the garlic and ginger.
2. Mix them using a whisk with the soy sauce and vinegar.
3. Whisk as you add the oil.
4. Lastly, add the pepper and sriracha if desired to serve.

Balsamic Vinaigrette

Servings: 8
Time Required: 10 minutes

Essential Ingredients:

- Balsamic vinegar (.5 cup/120 ml)
- Garlic clove (1)
- Dry mustard (1 tsp.)
- Salt & pepper
- Olive oil – EVOO – extra-virgin (120 ml/.5 cup)

Prep Method:

1. Mince the garlic, measure the fixings, and whisk in a mixing container.
2. Continue whisking for better results and serve.

Citrus Vinaigrette

Servings: 16
Time Required: 6 minutes

Essential Ingredients:

- Shallot (1 small)
- Extra-virgin olive oil (.75 cup/175 ml)
- Vinegar - lemon-flavored white balsamic/white wine/champagne vinegar (.25 cup/60 ml)
- Fresh orange juice (5 tbsp.)
- Lemon zest - may omit if using lemon-flavored vinegar (.25 tsp.)
- Black pepper & salt (to your liking)

Prep Method:

1. First, do the prep by finely mincing the garlic and zesting the lemon (if using). Prepare the orange juice.
2. Mix it thoroughly in a jar with a lid. Add pepper and salt as desired, shake again and serve.

Part 4: Dessert & Beverage Specialties

Enjoy the selections in this segment anytime!

Chapter 10: Diabetic Desserts

Cakes

Cappuccino Cupcake Delight

Servings: Varies
Time Required: 35 minutes (+) cool down time

Essential Ingredients:

- Sugar (1.5 cups)
- Baking soda (1 tsp.)
- A.P. flour (2 cups)
- Baking cocoa (.5 cup)
- Salt (.5 tsp.)
- Prune baby food (.5 cup)
- Instant coffee granules (.25 cup)
- Hot water (.5 cup)
- Eggs (2)
- Canola oil (.25 cup)
- Vanilla extract (2 tsp.)
- Whipped topping - reduced-fat (1.5 cups)
- Additional baking cocoa

Prep Method:

1. Place paper liners in the muffin cups.
2. Thoroughly combine/whisk the flour with baking soda, sugar, cocoa, and salt.
3. Dissolve the coffee in hot water. Set aside.
4. Whisk the eggs with the oil, vanilla, baby food, and coffee mixture. Gradually stir into the dry fixings - just until moistened. Fill the cups 2/3 full.
5. Bake at 350° Fahrenheit or 177 ° Celsius until a toothpick comes out clean (18-20 min.).
6. Cool them for ten minutes. Then remove them from the pans to the countertop on racks to thoroughly cool.
7. Ice the cupcakes with whipped topping and a sprinkle of cocoa right before serving. Refrigerate the leftovers for later.

Cookies & Fudge

Banana Chocolate Chip Cookies

Servings: 36 cookies
Time Required: 30-35 minutes

Essential Ingredients:

- Un-chilled butter (.33 cup)
- Sugar or a preferred equivalent (.5 cup)
- Un-chilled egg (1 large)
- Vanilla extract (.5 tsp.)
- Mashed ripe banana (.5 cup)
- A.P. flour (1.25 cups)
- Bak. powder (1 tsp.)
- Salt (.25 tsp.)
- Bak. soda (.125 tsp.)
- Semisweet chocolate chips (1 cup)

Prep Method:

1. Mix the sugar with the butter until fluffy. Whisk and add in the egg, banana, and vanilla.
2. Fully whisk the dry fixings (flour, salt, baking powder, & baking soda).
3. Slowly add the dry into the first mixture. Fold in the chips of chocolate.
4. Drop by tablespoonfuls about two inches apart onto baking trays coated with cooking oil spray.

5. Bake at 350° Fahrenheit/177 ° Celsius until the edges are browned (13-16 min.). Transfer the pans to wire racks to cool.
6. Serve and enjoy them anytime.

Carrot Cookie Bites

Servings: 7 dozen
Time Required: 25 minutes

Essential Ingredients:

- Shortening (.66 cup)
- Brown sugar - tightly packed (1 cup)
- Room temp large eggs (2)
- Buttermilk (.5 cup)
- Vanilla extract (1 tsp.)
- A.P. flour (2 cups)
- Salt (.5 tsp.)
- Bak. soda (.25 tsp.)
- Ground cloves (.25 tsp.)
- Bak. powder (.25 tsp.)
- Ground nutmeg (.25 tsp.)
- Cinnamon (1 tsp.)
- Shredded carrots (1 cup)
- Oats - Quick-cooking type (2 cups)
- Pecans (.5 cup)

Prep Method:

1. Combine the shortening with the brown sugar until light and fluffy (5-7 min.). Whisk and mix in the eggs with the buttermilk and vanilla. Whisk the flour with the salt, baking powder, cinnamon, cloves, baking soda, and nutmeg. Slowly mix it into the creamed mixture.

2. Chop and mix in the pecans, carrots, and oats.
3. Scoop and drop the dough (1 tsp. each) onto ungreased baking trays (2 in. apart).
4. Set the timer to bake at 375° Fahrenheit or 191° Celsius until lightly browned (6-8 min.). Place the pans onto wire racks to cool.

Chocolate Kiss & Peanut Butter Cookie Treats

Servings: 2 ½ dozen
Time Required: 30 minutes (+) cooling time

Essential Ingredients:

- Peanut butter (1 cup)
- Vanilla extract (1 tsp.)
- Room temperature egg (1 large)
- Sugar (1 cup)
- Milk chocolate kisses (30)

Prep Method:

1. Warm the oven to reach 350° Fahrenheit/177 ° Celsius.
2. Cream the sugar with the peanut butter until it's fluffy and light. Whisk the vanilla and egg, mixing them into the batter.
3. Spin the mixture into 1.25-inch balls. Now, place them two inches apart onto ungreased cookie trays. Bake until the tops are slightly cracked (10-13 min.).
4. Promptly push one of the chocolate kisses into the center of each cookie.
5. Cool the cookies for about five minutes before removing them from the pans to wire racks.

Easy & Light Cookie Cut-Outs

Servings: 24
Time Required: 25 minutes

Essential Ingredients:

- Unchilled butter (.25 cup)
- Sugar (.5 cup)
- Brown sugar - packed (.5 cup)
- Canola oil (2 tbsp.)
- Egg (1)
- Vanilla extract (.25 tsp.)
- A.P. flour (1.5 cups)
- Salt (.25 tsp.)
- Baking soda (.125 tsp.)

Variety Options:
- Yellow and red food coloring
- Beaten egg white
- Popsicle or lollipop sticks

Prep Method:

1. Beat the butter with both types of sugars until crumbly (2 min.). Whisk and mix in the egg, oil, and vanilla. Whisk the flour with baking soda and salt. Gradually add it to the mixture.
2. Lightly flour a work surface and divide the dough in half.
3. Roll one piece of the dough into 1/4-inch thickness.

4. Cut with a floured three-inch cookie cutter. Arrange the cookies one inch apart on baking sheets coated with cooking spray. Repeat until all the dough is used.
5. Bake at 350° Fahrenheit or 177 ° Celsius until set (5-6 min.). Cool the cookies for one minute before removing from the pans to wire racks.
6. Decorate as desired.

Molasses-Crackle Cookies

Servings: 2 ½ dozen
Time Required: 30 minutes (+) chilling time

Essential Ingredients:

- Canola oil (.25 cup)
- Egg (1 large)
- Sugar (.66 cup)
- Molasses (.33 cup)
- Ground cloves (.25 tsp.)
- Flour - white whole wheat used (2 cups)
- Bak. soda (1.5 tsp.)
- Ground ginger (.25 tsp.)
- Cinnamon (1 tsp.)
- Salt (.5 tsp.)
- Confectioners' sugar (1 tbsp.)

Prep Method:

1. Mix the sugar with the oil until blended. Whisk and mix in the egg and molasses.
2. Whisk the flour with the salt, cloves, baking soda, ginger, and cinnamon. Mix it into the sugar mixture.
3. Cover the container and put it into the refrigerator to chill for a minimum of two hours.
4. Warm the oven temperature to reach 350° Fahrenheit or 177 ° Celsius.
5. Shape the dough into one-inch balls and roll them in confectioners' sugar.

6. Arrange them about two inches apart onto baking trays coated with cooking spray.
7. Flatten them slightly to bake for seven to nine minutes or until they're firm. Scoop them at that time to finish cooling them on a wire rack.
8. Serve as desired.

Peanut Butter & Oatmeal Cookies

Servings: 24
Time Required: 20 minutes

Essential Ingredients:

- Peanut butter - chunky-style (.5 cup)
- Brown sugar - packed (.5 cup)
- Egg (1 large)
- Quick-cooking oats (1.25 cups)
- Baking soda (.5 tsp.)

Prep Method:

1. Preheat the oven to 350° Fahrenheit/177 ° Celsius.
2. Spritz the baking trays with a bit of oil spray as needed.
3. Combine the brown sugar and peanut butter, mixing until fluffy.
4. Whisk and mix in the egg. Fold in the oats and baking soda to the creamed mixture.
5. Thoroughly combine and drop by tablespoonfuls two inches apart onto the prepared cookie trays.
6. Flatten each one slightly. Bake for six to eight minutes and cool over wire racks. Store them in a cookie jar.

Bar Type Cakes

Almond Espresso Bars

Servings: 4 dozen
Time Required: 35 minutes (+) chilling time

Essential Ingredients:

- Room temp butter (.25 cup)
- Brown sugar - packed (1 cup)
- Brewed espresso (.5 cup)
- Egg (1 large)
- Self-rising flour (1.5 cups)
- Chopped slivered almonds - toasted (.75 cup)
- Ground cinnamon (.5 tsp.)

The Glaze:
- Confectioners' sugar (1.5 cups)
- Water (3 tbsp.)
- Almond extract (.75 tsp.)
- Slivered almonds - toasted (.25 cup)
- Needed: 15x10x1-in. baking pan

Prep Method:

1. Mix the butter with the brown sugar and espresso till fully mixed.
2. Whisk and stir in the egg. Whisk the flour with the cinnamon, slowly adding it to the creamed mixture. Chop and mix in the almonds.

3. Spread them onto a greased baking pan to cook at 350° Fahrenheit or 177° Celsius until lightly browned (18-22 min.).
4. In another mixing container, combine the water with the confectioners' sugar and extract until creamy smooth.
5. Spread the mixture over warm bars and sprinkle with slivered almonds. Cool on a wire rack.
6. Slice them into bars to serve.

Fudge

Servings: 40 squares
Time Required: 5 minutes (+) chilling time (2 hr.)

Essential Ingredients:

- Coconut butter (1.5 cups)
- Coconut milk – full-fat suggested (13.66 fl. oz. can)
- Bittersweet chocolate chips (10 oz.)
- Optional Topping: Flaked/coarse sea salt
- Also Suggested: 8 by 8-inch baking pan

Prep Method:

1. Line the baking pan with a layer of foil or waxed paper.
2. Now, melt the coconut butter in a saucepan using the low-temperature setting.
3. Mix in the chips and milk. Let the mixture simmer, frequently stirring until the chocolate has melted.
4. Empty the batter into the prepared baking pan. Drizzle with sea salt and pop it into the fridge until it's set (2 hrs.). Slice and serve.

Pies & Tarts

Apple Pie

Servings: 8
Time Required: 20 minutes (+) chilling time

Essential Ingredients:

- Ground cinnamon (.5 tsp.)
- S.F. lemon gelatin (0.3 oz. pkg.)
- Ground nutmeg (.25 tsp.)
- Water - divided (.1.75 cups)
- Tart apples (5 medium - peeled and sliced)
- S. F. - cook-&-serve vanilla pudding mix (0.8 oz. pkg.)
- Chopped nuts (.5 cup)
- Graham cracker crust - reduced-fat (6 oz.)
- Optional: Whipped topping

Prep Method:

1. Combine the gelatin with the nutmeg, cinnamon, and 1.5 cups water. Add the apples into an oversized saucepan – waiting for it to come to a boil.
2. Now, simmer it covered until the apples are tender (5 min.).
3. Whisk the pudding mix and the rest of the water. Stir it into the apple mixture. Cook until thickened, occasionally stirring (1 min.).

4. Remove the pan and mix in the nuts. Add it to the prepared crust.
5. Refrigerate for at least two hours before serving with whipped topping or as desired.

Deconstructed Raspberry Pie

Servings: 4
Required Time: 20 minutes

Essential Ingredients:

- Melted butter (2 tbsp.)
- Sugar or sugar equivalent (2 tsp.)
- Graham cracker crumbs (.5 cup)
- Whipped cream in a can (4 tbsp.)
- Baking cocoa (.25 tsp.)
- Fresh raspberries (2-2/3 cups)
- Also Needed: 8x6-in. rectangle baking dish

Prep Method:

1. Toss the sugar with the raspberries and set aside for now.
2. Use another bowl to mix the butter with the cracker crumbs. Press the mixture into the ungreased baking sheet.
3. Bake at 350° Fahrenheit/177 ° Celsius until they are browned to your liking (5-6 min.). Cool them thoroughly on a wire rack before breaking them into large chunks.
4. Portion ½ of the graham cracker pieces into four dessert dishes: Top with raspberries (1/3 cup).
5. Continue the layers, topping each one with one tablespoon of whipped cream and a sprinkle of cocoa.

Ginger Plum Tart

Servings: 8
Time Required: 30-35 minutes

Essential Ingredients:

- Refrigerated pie crust (12-inch sheet)
- Cornstarch (1 tbsp.)
- Sugar (3 tbsp.)
- Crystallized ginger (2 tsp.)
- Egg white (1 large)
- Water (1 tbsp.)

Prep Method:

1. Slice the plums and finely chop the ginger.
2. Prepare a cookie tray using a sheet of parchment paper.
3. Set the oven to 400° Fahrenheit/204° Celsius.
4. Unroll the crust and place it on the prepared tray.
5. Toss the plums with cornstarch and sugar. Place them over the crust to within two inches of its edges and sprinkle with ginger. Fold the crust edge over plums, pleating as you go.
6. Whisk the egg white and water, making an egg wash to brush over the folded crust. Now dust it with the remainder of the sugar.

7. Lastly, bake till the crust is nicely browned (18-25 min.). Wait for it to cool in the pan.
8. Once it's cooled, serve as desired.

Key Lime Pie

Servings: 8
Required Time: 20 minutes (+) chilling time

Essential Ingredients:

- Lime gelatin - sugar-free (0.3 oz. pkg.)
- Boiling water (.25 cup)
- Key lime yogurt (2 containers @ 6 oz. each)
- Frozen & thawed whipped topping - fat-free (8 oz. carton)
- Graham cracker crust - reduced-fat (8-inch)

Prep Method:

1. Prepare a big mixing container and add boiling water to the gelatin. Whisk it until it is liquified (2 min.).
2. Whisk in the yogurt and gently fold in the whipped topping. Dump it into the crust.
3. Pop it into the fridge with a cover until it's set (2 hrs.).

Ribbon Pudding Pie

Servings: 8
Time Required: 20 minutes (+) chilling time

Essential Ingredients:

- Cold fat-free milk - divided (4 cups)
- Sugar-free instant vanilla pudding mix (1 oz. pkg.)
- Reduced-fat graham cracker crust (6 oz.)
- S.F. instant butterscotch pudding mix (1 oz. pkg.)
- S.F. instant chocolate pudding mix (1.4 oz. pkg.)
Optional:
- Whipped topping
- Finely chopped pecans

Prep Method:

1. Whisk the milk (1.33 cups) and vanilla pudding mix for two minutes. Spread into crust.
2. In a separate mixing container, whisk another 1.33 cups of milk with the butterscotch pudding mix for two minutes. Carefully spoon over the vanilla layer, spreading evenly.
3. Use an additional bowl to whisk the rest of the milk (1.33 cups) and chocolate

pudding. Mix for two minutes. Carefully spread over the top.
4. Refrigerate until set, at least ½ hour.
5. Top it off using whipped topping and pecans to your liking.

Tasty Sweet Treats

No-Bake Peanut Butter Treats

Servings: 15
Time Required: 10 minutes

Essential Ingredients:

- Chunky peanut butter (.33 cup)
- Honey (.25 cup)
- Vanilla extract (.5 tsp.)
- Quick-cooking oats (.33 cup)
- Nonfat dry milk powder (.33 cup)
- Graham cracker crumbs (2 tbsp.)

Prep Method:

1. Cream the peanut butter with the honey and vanilla. Mix in the milk powder, oats, and cracker crumbs.
2. Shape the mixture into one-inch balls. Cover and pop them into the fridge until it's time to serve.

Sour Cream Bavarian

Servings: 8 – 1.25 cups of sauce
Time Required: 15 minutes (+) chilling time

Essential Ingredients:

- Unflavored gelatin (1 envelope)
- Water - cold (.75 cup)
- Sugar (.66 cup)
- Vanilla extract (1 tsp.)
- Sour cream - fat-free (1 cup)
- Whipped topping - fat-free (2 cups)

The Sauce:
- Frozen sweetened raspberries or sliced strawberries - thawed (10 oz. pkg.)
- Cornstarch (1 tbsp.)
- Sugar (1 tbsp.)

Prep Method:

1. Prepare a saucepan and sprinkle the gelatin into cold water. Wait for one minute. Add sugar and warm it while stirring using the low temperature setting until the gelatin and sugar are liquified.
2. Transfer the mixture to a bowl. Whisk in sour cream and vanilla and refrigerate it for ten minutes.
3. Mix in the whipped topping. Empty it into a four-cup mold coated with

cooking spray. Refrigerate, covered, until firm, about four hours.
4. Prepare the sauce by draining the berries, reserving the syrup. Pour in enough water into the syrup to measure ¾ cup.
5. Use a small saucepan to mix the cornstarch with the sugar and syrup mixture until smooth. Once boiling, simmer and stir until thickened (2 min.). Cool slightly. Stir in drained berries and refrigerate until serving.
6. To serve, unmold dessert onto a serving plate. Serve with sauce.

Delicious Frozen Treats
Apricot Lemon Fruit Pops

Servings: 6
Time Required: 15 minutes (+) freezing time

Essential Ingredients:

- Orange juice (.25 cup)
- Grated lemon zest (1 tsp.)
- Sugar (4 tsp.)
- Lemon juice (.25 cup)
- Fresh apricots (1 cup/4-5 medium)
- Ice cubes (.5 cup)
  ****
- Optional: 1 teaspoon minced fresh mint (1 tsp.)
- Molds & sticks for the pops (6 @ 6 tbsp. each)

Prep Method:

1. Slice the apricots and make the juice and zest from the lemon.
2. Toss the first six fixings into a blender (up to the line**); cover and process until blended. Add in freshly minced mint.
3. Pour the mixture into molds and freeze until firm.

Berry Ice Pops

Servings: 10
Time Required: 10 minutes (+) Freezing time

Essential Ingredients:

- Whole milk - divided (1.75 cups)
- Honey (1-2 tbsp.)
- Vanilla extract (.25 tsp.)
- Blueberries - fresh (1 cup)
- Raspberries - fresh (1.5 cups)
- Paper cups or freezer pop molds & sticks (10 @ about 6 tbsp. each)

Prep Method:

1. Pour the water into a safe container and warm ¼ cup of milk in the microwave. Stir in the honey and rest of the milk (1.5 cups), and vanilla.
2. Portion the berries into the molds and pour milk into the mixture. Place the tops onto the molds with holders.
3. Pop them in the freezer until they are solid to serve.

Berry Yogurt Swirls

Servings: 10 pops
Time Required: 15 minutes (+) freezing time

Essential Ingredients:

- Plastic or paper cups (10 @ 3 oz. each)
- Honey Greek yogurt - fat-free (2.75 cups)
- Fresh berries - mixed (1 cup)
- Water (.25 cup)
- Sugar (2 tbsp.)
- Wooden pop sticks (10)

Prep Method:

1. Fill each cup with yogurt (¼ cup).
2. Prepare the food processor. Toss in the berries, water, and sugar. Swirl it until the berries are thoroughly chopped.
3. Scoop 1.5 tablespoons of the berry mixture into each cup. Gently stir using a popsicle stick to swirl.
4. Top each of the cups with foil and add the pop sticks in through foil. Freeze until they are solid.
5. Grab any time for a delicious treat!

Chocolate Hazelnut & Soy Pops

Servings: 8
Time Required: 10 minutes (+) freezing time

Essential Ingredients:

- Soy milk - vanilla (1 cup)
- Milk – fat-free used (.5 cup)
- Vanilla Greek yogurt - fat-free (.75 cup)
- Nutella (1/3 cup)
- Paper cups/pop molds (8 @ 3 ounces each) & wooden pop sticks

Prep Method:

1. Pour the milk, yogurt, and Nutella into a blender.
2. Securely close the top and mix until it's creamy. Scoop it into the holders and seal the tops with foil, adding the sticks.
3. Freeze until firm.

Chunky Banana Cream Freeze

Servings: 3 cups
Time Required: 15 minutes (+) freezing time

Essential Ingredients:

- Bananas - peeled & frozen (5 medium)
- Unsweetened coconut - finely shredded (2 tbsp.)
- Almond milk (.33 cup)
- Vanilla extract (1 tsp.)
- Creamy peanut butter (2 tbsp.)
- Chopped walnuts (.25 cup)
- Raisins (3 tbsp.)

Prep Method:

1. Place the bananas, peanut butter, milk, vanilla, and coconut in a food processor. Close the lid and blend the mixture.
2. Pour it into a freezer container, and fold in the walnuts and raisins. Freeze for two to four hours before serving.

Patriotic Pops

Servings: 12
Time Required: 15 minutes (+) freezing time

Essential Ingredients:

- Vanilla yogurt - divided (1.75 cups)
- Honey - divided (2 tbsp.)
- Fresh strawberries - sliced & divided (1.25 cups)
- Frozen or fresh blueberries - thawed & divided (1.25 cups)
- Freezer popsicle molds/paper cups (12 @ 3 oz. each) & wooden pop sticks

Prep Method:

1. Measure and add one tablespoon honey, two tablespoons yogurt, and one cup strawberries in a blender. Place the lid on tightly and process until blended. Pour it into a small, holding container.
2. Chop the rest of the strawberries and add them to the mixture.
3. Use a blender to process the rest of the honey with two tablespoons of yogurt and one cup of blueberries. Transfer them to another container. Fold in the rest of the blueberries.
4. Prepare the molds. Scoop the strawberry mixture (1 tbsp.), yogurt (2 tbsp.), and blueberry mixture (1 tbsp.).

5. Top with the popsicle sticks or cover the cups with a layer of foil. Freeze until firm.

Soft-Serve Raspberry-Banana

Servings: 2 ½ cups
Time Required: 10 minutes (+) freezing time

Essential Ingredients:

- Ripe bananas (4 medium)
- Fat-free plain yogurt (.5 cup)
- Maple syrup (1-2 tbsp.)
- Frozen unsweetened raspberries (.5 cup)
- Optional: Fresh raspberries

Prep Method:

1. Thinly slice the bananas and transfer them into a large plastic zipper-type freezer bag. Arrange the slices in a single layer; freeze overnight.
2. Finely chop the bananas in a food processor.
3. Mix in the yogurt, maple syrup, and raspberries. Pulse the mixture a few times just until smooth, scraping sides as needed.
4. Serve immediately, adding fresh berries as desired.

Rhubarb- Strawberry Ice Pops

Servings: 8
Time Required: 25 minutes (+) chilling time

Essential Ingredients:

- Chopped fresh or frozen rhubarb (3 cups)
- Sugar (.25 cup)
- Water (3 tbsp.)
- Yogurt - strawberry flavor (1 cup)
- Applesauce - unsweetened (.5 cup)
- Fresh strawberries (.25 cup)
- Optional: Red food coloring (2 drops)
- Paper cups/freezer pop molds (8 @ 3 ounces each) and wooden sticks

Prep Method:

1. Slice the rhubarb into ½-inch cuts and mix with the water and sugar in a big saucepan. Once boiling, reduce the temperature setting to simmer, uncovered, until thick and blended (10-15 min.).
2. Scoop out about 3/4 cup of the mixture into a bowl to cool. (Save the rest of the rhubarb another time.)
3. Add the applesauce, yogurt, and finely chopped strawberries to the container – stirring till it is thoroughly mixed – adding the food coloring if desired.

4. Fill each of the chosen holders with the rhubarb mixture (1/4 cup each).
5. Top the molds with holders and top cups with a layer of foil. Push the sticks through the foil. Then freeze them until they are solid to serve.

Strawberry Lemonade Popsicles

Servings: 6
Time Required: 5 minutes (+) chilling time

Essential Ingredients:

- Old-fashioned oats (.25 cup/22 g)
- Low fat cottage cheese (4 oz./115 g)
- Strawberries (1.5 lb./680 g)
- Lemon juice (4 oz./about 4 lemons/115 g)
- Liquid Stevia (5 drops)
- Essential: Food processor or high-powered blender

Prep Method:

1. Pulse the oats until they're powdery.
2. Add the cottage cheese, strawberries, stevia, and lemon juice.
3. Pulse the mixture until smooth. Don't add any liquid!
4. Prepare the six molds and freeze until firm (approx. 3 hrs.).

Strawberry Sorbet

Servings: 8
Time Required: 20 minutes (+) freezing time

Essential Ingredients:

- Strawberry sorbet (2 cups)
- Cold milk- fat-free (1 cup)
- Instant vanilla pudding mix - sugar-free (1 oz. pkg.)
- Reduced-fat whipped topping (frozen 8 oz. carton)
- Sliced fresh strawberries
- Also Suggested: 8x4-inch loaf pan

Prep Method:

1. Thaw the whipped topping.
2. Line the loaf pan with plastic wrap. Slightly soften the sorbet and add it to the pan. Freeze it for about 15 minutes.
3. Meanwhile, whisk the pudding mix with the milk for two minutes. It will be soft set soon (2 min.). Mix and add the thawed topping over the sorbet. Cover the container to freeze and set for four hours to overnight.
4. Transfer the pan to the countertop to slightly thaw before serving (10-15 min.). Flip and invert the dessert onto a plate. Discard the plastic and slice the

sorbet. Lastly, slice the strawberries and sprinkle them over the top to serve.

Chapter 11: Diabetic Favorite Beverages

Agua-&-Strawberry Fresca

Servings: 6 cups
Time Required: 5 minutes

Essential Ingredients:

- Fresh strawberries (2 cups)
- Water (4 cups)
- Kosher salt (1 pinch)
- Optional: Honey or another sweetener (1 tbsp.)

Prep Method:

1. Toss the strawberries, water, salt, and sweetener into your processor or blender.
2. Purée till the mixture is velvety.
3. Serve in chilled glasses.

Basil Lemonade

Servings: 6
Time Required: 20 minutes

Essential Ingredients:

- Fresh lemon juice (1.25 cups/+ more for garnishing/from about 8 lemons)
- Honey/agave syrup (.5 cup)
- Packed fresh basil leaves (1 cup + more to garnish)
- Water (3 cups - cold)
- Ice cubes (1 cup)

Prep Method:

1. Load the blender with the basil, honey, and lemon juice, mixing until it's creamy smooth. Pour it into a large jar or pitcher using a sieve to strain.
2. Pour in the water and pop it into the fridge until time to serve.
3. Enjoy it over ice and a lemon slice with a couple of basil leaves.

Citrusy Spa Water

Servings: 6
Time Required: 5 minutes

Essential Ingredients:

- Lemon (1)
- Lime (1)
- Orange (1)
- Pink grapefruit (1)
- Water (6 cups)

Prep Method:

1. Slice each piece of fruit into halves.
2. Juice all the fruit into a measuring cup and trash the rinds.
3. Pour the juice through a strainer and into a pitcher that will hold at least 8 cups of liquid.
4. Add the water and stir well to serve.

Healthy Fruit Sparklers

Servings: 5
Time Required: 5 minutes

Essential Ingredients:

- Ice cubes (1 cup)
- Low-calorie grape/cranberry or pomegranate juice (3 cups)
- Sparkling water (3 cups)
- Optional: Halved fresh cranberries, grapes, or raspberries (.75 cup)

Prep Method:

1. Half fill six tall glasses with ice cubes.
2. Portion the grape juice evenly between the glasses.
3. Pour sparkling water into the glasses, and gently stir.
4. Decorate with a few floating grapes in the drinks.

Lemon & Ginger Tea

Servings: 5
Time Required: 20 minutes

Essential Ingredients:

- Water (6 cups)
- Sugar substitute (1 tbsp.)
- Lemon peel (8 strips)
- Fresh ginger (2-inch piece)
- Green tea bags (3)
- Lemon (5 slices)

Prep Method:

1. Slice the lemon strips (2.5 x 1-inches). Peel and thinly slice the ginger.
2. Prepare a saucepan of water and toss in the strips of lemon and ginger. Lower the temperature setting, and simmer for ten minutes. Discard the ginger and lemon.
3. Toss the tea bags in a teapot and promptly add to the simmering lemon-infused water. Place a lid on the pot and steep (1-3 min.).
4. Gently squeeze the bags and enjoy immediately.
5. Sweeten to your liking to serve.

Sunrise Peach Refresher

Servings: 4
Time Required: 5 minutes

Essential Ingredients:

- Ice - divided (2 cups)
- Diet cranberry juice drink - divided (1.33 cups)
- Peach nectar, divided (1.33 cups)
- Mint (4 sprigs)
- Quartered orange (4 slices)

Prep Method:

1. Put ½ cup of ice into each of the glasses.
2. Add 1/3 cup portions of cranberry juice and peach nectar to each glass.
3. Top them off with mint springs and orange slices.

Chapter 12: Diabetic Mocktails & Cocktails

Blood Orange Margaritas

Servings: 6
Time Required: 15 minutes

Essential Ingredients:

- Triple Sec (.25 cup)
- Grated blood orange zest (1 tbsp.)
- Optional: Kosher salt (1 tbsp.)
- Blood orange juice (1 cup)
- White tequila (1 cup)
- Lime juice (.5 cup + 1 lime wedge)
- Simple syrup (2 tbsp.)
- Ice cubes (1 cup)

To Garnish:
- Blood orange slices (6 slices)
- Lime slices (12 slices)

Prep Method:

1. Chill the tequila and orange juice.
2. Sprinkle zested orange over a small plate and toss with salt (if using).
3. Now, combine the tequila with the lime juice, simple syrup, orange juice, and Triple Sec in a pitcher.

4. Prepare the glasses by lightly rubbing the rims with a lime wedge - dip in the zest (or zest-salt mixture).
5. Fill each of the glasses with ice and pour in about ½ cup of the margarita mixture into each. Top it off with lime or orange slices as preferred.
6. The recipe contains ½ fruit and 1 alcohol equivalent point for the diabetic exchange

Ginger-Lemon Kombucha Cocktail

Servings: 1
Time Required: 5 minutes

Essential Ingredients:

- Lemon-ginger kombucha (.5 cup)
- Vodka (1.5 oz.)
- Lemon juice (1 tbsp.)
- Ice cubes
- Lemon slice (1)
- Mint (3 leaves)
- Also Needed: Jar with a tight-fitting lid or a cocktail shaker

Prep Method:

1. Prepare the drink in the shaker/jar, combine kombucha, vodka, and lemon juice. Close it tightly and shake.
2. Now, add mint leaves to an ice-filled medium glass. Add the cocktail ingredients, then top with a lemon slice.

Hot Bourbon Cocoa

Servings: 6
Time Required: 15 minutes

Essential Ingredients:

- Chocolate pieces – bittersweet used (.5 cup)
- Unsweetened cocoa powder (.25 cup)
- Milk – fat-free (4 cups)
- Honey (2 tbsp.)
- Bourbon (.5 cup/4 oz.)
- Ground cinnamon (1 pinch)

Prep Method:

1. Melt the chocolate pieces and cocoa powder in a saucepan.
2. Whisk in the milk (3.5 cups) and the honey.
3. Simmer using the medium-temperature setting, just until boiling and chocolate pieces are melted, whisking continuously. Mix in the bourbon.
4. For a frothy topper, pour the rest of the milk (.5 cup) into a bowl. Microwave till it is warm (20-30 seconds). Beat with a whisk until frothy.
5. Serve the cocoa with a frothy topper and a sprinkle of cinnamon or more cocoa powder.

Mojito Mocktails

Servings: 4
Time Required: 10 minutes

Essential Ingredients:

- Fresh mint leaves (.5 cup – packed)
- Lime for juice (6 for .75 cup)
- Simple syrup (.75 cup **)
- Lime zest (2 strips - 2-inch)
- Ice cubes (4 cups)
- Sparkling water (2 cups)
- To Garnish: Lime slices (4 slices @ ¼-inch thickness) & mint sprigs (4)

Prep Method:

1. Make your simple syrup: **Pour one cup of sugar into a medium saucepan, frequently stirring until it's liquified. Cool the mixture for ½ hour and refrigerate until cold (1 hr.). The syrup can be stored in the fridge, covered, for up to six months.
2. Combine the lime juice with the mint leaves, simple syrup, and lime zest in a pitcher. Lightly crush the mint and zest.
3. Toss in the cubed ice and sparkling water, thoroughly stirring to serve.
4. Portion the drink into four glasses. Add a few lime slices and mint sprigs to top it off.

Spicy Ginger-Pineapple Mocktail

Servings: 3
Time Required: 10 minutes

Essential Ingredients:

- Pineapple (2 cups – chopped + more to top)
- Jalapeno/serrano pepper (1)
- Unpeeled fresh ginger (2-inch piece)
- Water (.25 cup)
- Cubed ice
- Optional: Pure maple syrup (1 tbsp.)
- Seltzer (.75 cup)

Prep Method:

3. Prep the ingredients. Remove the seeds and slice the pepper.
4. Load the blender with the water, ginger, jalapeno, and pineapple to mix using the high-speed setting (30 sec.).
5. Use a fine-mesh strainer to discard the solids.
6. Now fill the glass (12 oz.) with ice and strained juice (1/3 cup), syrup,
7. and top with the seltzer.
8. Stir and garnish with pineapple as desired.

Spicy Hot Cider & Apple Brandy

Servings: 8
Time Required: 25 minutes

Essential Ingredients:

- Apple cider/apple juice (8 cups)
- Whole allspice berries (4)
- Whole cloves (4)
- Whole cardamom seeds (4)
- Cinnamon (4 sticks)
- Calvados - brandy (1 cup)

Prep Method:

1. You are provided with two fruits on the diabetic exchange.
2. Combine the cider or juice with the cloves, cardamom, allspice, and cinnamon sticks in a large saucepan.
3. Simmer for 20 minutes and strain out the spices
4. Stir in the Calvados or brandy.
5. Serve piping-hot in heavy mugs.

The Final Words to Satisfaction

I hope you have enjoyed the recipes provided for you in your copy of the *Diabetic Cook for the Newly Diagnosed*. I tried to pack it full of easy recipes for you and your family to enjoy from morning to night. Now, all you need to do is gather a shopping list and head to the market.

If you really want to prepare some easy snacks or if you are on-the-run most of the time; let's continue with these easy ones for now to enjoy anytime. You can also save time by preparing some of the treats in advance - leaving them readily available in the fridge!

Don't worry, your family will also devour the special snacks without realizing how much better their health can become!

Here is a few to begin your journey.

A Healthy Avocado Bowl
1. Slice an avocado in half.
2. Then garnish ½ with salsa (1-2 tbsp.) and shredded cheese (1 tsp.).
3. Enjoy right from the avocado skin.

Avocado Toast

1. Use these toppings for the toast.
2. Toasted whole grain bread (1 slice).
3. Top it with ¼ of a small avocado.
4. Optionally garnish it using pumpkin or sunflower seeds (1 tsp.).

Nut Butter & Sliced Apples

1. Select a medium apple and cut it into halves.
2. Then, scoop it into peanut or your favorite nut butter (approx. 1 tbsp.).
3. Dust it with a sprinkle of cinnamon as desired.

Nut Butter Whole Grain Toast

1. Use one slice of bread, toast it, and top with peanut or another chosen nut butter (1 tbsp.).
2. Enjoy every morsel.

Guacamole & Raw Veggies

1. First prepare the chosen veggies (radishes, red bell pepper, or cucumber).
2. Dip the raw veggie sticks in ¼ cup healthy guacamole.

Hard-Boiled Eggs

1. Are you looking for a quick protein-packed snack? Prepare several eggs and leave them unpeeled in the refrigerator.
2. Optionally, serve with a dusting of pepper, salt, and hot sauce as desired.

Celery & Peanut Butter

1. Prepare several sticks of lettuce with a scoop of peanut butter (1 tsp. each).
2. You can also dot with several raisins.

Cucumber Boats

1. Slice a small cucumber in half lengthwise and scoop out the seeds.
2. Fill one cucumber half with chicken or tuna salad (1/2 cup).
3. Then enjoy the treat!

Edamame Favorite

1. Take one cup steamed edamame in the pods.
2. Sprinkle them using a bit of reduced-sodium soy sauce.

Fruit & Cheese

1. Choose one small piece of fruit such as a plum or clementine or plum.

2. Add a portion of string cheese for a grand snack.

Green Wrap

1. Prep the chosen veggie.
2. Then spread pieces of avocado (1/4 of 1) over a (whole-wheat tortilla 6-inch).
3. Garnish it with a portion of fresh greens such as arugula or spinach.
4. Then wrap tightly and dive in.

Ranch & Raw Veggies

1. Thoroughly rinse, dry, and slice the chosen raw veggie sticks (your option).
2. Dip them into a low-cal ranch dressing (2 tbsp.).

Savory Cottage Cheese

1. Rinse the cucumber or tomato.
2. Chop it as desired.
3. Sprinkle it over a dish of low-fat cottage cheese (.5 cup) to serve.

Sweet Cottage Cheese

1. Choose peaches or pineapple (chopped). You can also choose berries in ¼ cup portions.
2. Prepare ½ cup pf cottage cheese, top it off, and enjoy.

Cream Cheese & Cucumber Sandwiches

1. Rinse and slice the cucumber into two sandwich-type slices.
2. Make six of them and spread a layer (1 tsp.) of cream cheese between each 'sandwich'.

Hummus & Raw Veggies

1. Grab a few raw veggies such as red bell pepper, cucumber, or radishes.
2. Dip them into ¼ cup of hummus.

Peanut Butter & Chocolate

1. Choose two (sugar-free) mini 'Hershey's Special Dark Chocolate' bars.
2. Dip them into peanut butter (2 tsp.).

Peanut Butter Sandwich Crackers

1. Use two whole grain crackers for each sandwich.
2. Smear a cracker with a nut butter such as peanut (1 tsp.).
3. Make two 'sandwiches' total.

Popcorn Favorite

1. First, have some fun and pop the corn (about 2 cups).
2. Drizzle olive oil (1 tsp.) over the air-popped corn with a sprinkle of your favorite spice.

3. Choose from pepper or salt. Or select another spice blend such as lemon pepper, Old Bay, Cajun seasoning, etc.

Roasted Chickpeas

1. Simply roast and grab about ¼ cup of chickpeas.

Trail Mix

1. Combine some dried fruit such as raisins with a few chopped nuts, or healthy seeds such as sunflower or pumpkin.
2. Scoop about one tablespoon of each item chosen into a bowl to enjoy.

Turkey Cheese Wrap

1. Visit your local deli and purchase some turkey.
2. Make a 'wrap' with the meat, adding, sliced cheese.
3. Top it off with your favorite fresh greens such as arugula or spinach.
4. Close and tightly wrap to enjoy.

Savory Yogurt Parfait

1. Rinse and prepare about ¼ cup of cucumber.
2. Scoop nonfat plain Greek yogurt (about ½ cup) into a serving dish.

3. Sprinkle the cucumber over the top a spritz with olive oil (1 tsp.) and a dusting of pepper and salt to your liking.

Yogurt Parfait

1. Measure about ½ cup Greek yogurt (nonfat and plain) into a serving glass.
2. Toss it with chopped nuts (1 tbsp.) and chopped fruit or berries (¼ cup).

How about that for a snack? Now you can decide which meal best suits you as you plan the next phase of your newly diagnosed illness.

Lastly, if you were pleased with the contents of this book could you make a brief reply to Amazon. It is always appreciated!

Printed in Great Britain
by Amazon